Reflections of the Heart

What Our Animal Companions Tell Us

Deborah DeMoss Smith

HOWELL
BOOK
HOUSE

Howell Book House
Published by Wiley Publishing, Inc., Hoboken, New Jersey
Published simultaneously in Canada

For general information about our other products and services, please contact our Customer Care Department within the United States at (800) 762-2974, outside the United States at (317) 572-3993 or fax (317) 572-4002.

Wiley also publishes its books in a variety of electronic formats. Some content that appears in print may not be available in electronic books. For more information about Wiley products, visit our web site at www.wiley.com.

Library of Congress Cataloging-in-Publication Data:

Smith, Deborah DeMoss, date.
    Reflections of the heart : what our animal companions tell us / by Deborah DeMoss Smith. — 1st ed.
        p. cm.
    Includes bibliographical references.
    ISBN 0-7645-5949-4 (alk. paper)
  1. Callahan, Sharon. 2. Animal communicators—California—Biography. 3. Human-animal communication. I. Title.
    SF411.45.C36S65 2004
    636.088'7'019—dc22

                                                                    2004009475

Printed in the United States of America

10 9 8 7 6 5 4 3 2 1

This book is dedicated to Jerry, Order of the Orange.
His resolute and loving presence inspired me to
give those without a voice, a voice.

Love is a mirror, it reflects
only your essence,
if you have the courage
to look in its face.

Rumi, c.1248

Contents

Foreword

f one would have told me years ago, as a veterinarian committed to medicine and science, that one of my most respected and valued friends, would be an animal communicator and flower essence developer, I would have dismissed them as *not having both oars in the water.*

However, as my mind has opened to the awareness that there are many approaches to helping animals, people and the planet heal, I have realized that I should not be attached to a limited number of modalities; but instead I should be open to whatever can be of benefit to all beings. This journey has led me to acupuncture, herbal medicine, chiropractic, mind-body medicine and other therapies.

Yet, in 1999, when I first met Animal Intuitive Sharon Callahan at the San Francisco Humane Society conference, animal communication and flower essences were still a bit over the top for me to grasp from a scientific background.

But, as I got to know Sharon and her work better, that soon changed. For, in time, I had the opportunity to see her undeniable connection with animals and their caretakers, one that was grounded in an impressive, healing ability to communicate with both.

I am forever grateful to know Sharon professionally and personally, one who shares my belief that animals are sentient beings rich in body, mind and soul. Savor the stories of the animals and their messages, their human companions and the woman who connects them all with love and wisdom in *Reflections of the Heart: What Our Animal Companions Tell Us.* May this book bring light into you and your animal companions' lives.

—Allen M. Schoen, M.S., D.V.M.
Author of *Kindred Spirits: How the Remarkable Bond
Between Humans and Animals Can Change the Way We Live*

Introduction

W *hen our family* veterinarian announced a decade ago that physical tests had not unraveled the reasons for our cat's deteriorating physical condition, she suggested I call an animal intuitive whose work she respected. Sharon Callahan, she said, had more than a way with animals; she had a direct line to them, an awareness that allowed her to communicate with them emotionally, mentally and spiritually. And unlike other animal communicators, she made her own healing flower essences for animals. I took the number and never regretted it.

Through her intuitive abilities, she was able, as Sharon explained, to merge with our feline Jerr-Berr, pick up his thoughts and mental images, and feel his emotions. It was like, she said, being so in tune with another, you know exactly what he or she is feeling and thinking.

The consultation, along with the prescribed flower essences, not only helped Jerr-Berr, but it also helped me to see my feline friend in a different light, one that reflected back on me. Through him, I learned about myself.

Jerr-Berr taught me using the language of reflection. That is what the animals in our lives do. As our mirrors, they show us, with their behaviors, emotions and attitudes, an honest picture of ourselves, allowing us to approach life more aware of our thoughts, feelings and actions, as well as our rich spiritual connection to one another.

Offering examples of mirroring, *Reflections of the Heart: What Our Animal Companions Tell Us* features the animal companions bees, cats, dogs, horses, parrots, rabbits, snakes and a turtle. Their true stories of loving service to their human partners will hopefully shine in your heart. And, that, I'm sure the animals would say, would be the fairest reflection of all.

1

THE ANIMAL BLESSING

"Dr. Dorian, do you believe animals talk?"
"I never heard one say anything," he replied.
"But that proves nothing. It is quite possible
that an animal has spoken civilly to me
and that I didn't catch the remark
because I wasn't paying attention."

Charlotte's Web, E. B. White

Bathed in the late autumn sunlight of Central Park, the woman sat cross-legged on the knoll, gently twisted like a soft New York pretzel. Her eyes surveyed the city's big expanse of recreational fields, tree-lined paths and wooden benches, all peppered with the sounds of people in play and private conversation. A long way from her home in Mt. Shasta, California, she was new to the many languages that wafted through the air. But she was not a novice to another kind of language that interlaced the buzz of the park, a language that went beyond the resonance of verbal words, but that no less communicated stories with rich images, thoughts and feelings.

As if on cue, two Airedales, their wiry tan and black coats recently washed, interrupted Sharon Callahan's contemplation as they strutted by with their human companions. As the frisky dogs sent a hey-aren't-we-having-fun message Sharon's way, she and her partner Purusha laughed. But the canines had more to say. Knowing the importance of reconnecting to nature, they wanted the woman who seemed so easily to tune into them to know that they were proud to be the catalyst for today's outing with their fellow city dwellers; they also wanted her to know they were just doing their jobs, for they took their service to their human friends to heart. As Sharon acknowledged their work, the boys sped off barking, headed toward some quick movements they'd eyed by a nearby tree.

As she closed her eyes and centered herself to meditate, other animals beckoned to this petite woman wrapped in the free-flowing purple top and soft black pants. The squirrels and birds, that so many New Yorkers care for with bread crumbs and peanuts, had something to add. Though they had no taste for the canine species' endless obsession for chasing, they did agree with the dogs in one way: they were glad to do their part in helping to bring people together to nurture life of all kinds, knowing that when people nurture others, they also nurture themselves. And since September 11, 2001, when the devastating collapse of the World Trade Center shook them all, that need was even greater than before.

Thanking them for their service, Sharon made a mental note to emphasize that in the homily today. She lay back on the sparsely grassed hillside and gazed into the pastel sky. In an hour she would be walking into a Manhattan church to give a homily and be an integral part of a special blessing. It would be another first for her: speaking to a large gathering in a structure that reminded her of another one she had walked away from years before. What a sense of humor the Universe had.

Though she'd grown up in a devout Irish Catholic home in San Francisco, she'd absconded from organized religion at the age of nine when, during a catechism class one afternoon after school, the priest stated (as if indeed it came straight from the Gospels), that not all of God's creations were equal in His sight. And though she'd be a teen before she followed her heart's decision to leave it all behind, she knew that the priest's words did not vibrate with what she felt, what she knew to be true: that some of our fellow beings are not only more than what they appear to be, but that they also communicate, speaking in a language beyond the expected barks, neighs, meows and chirps. No strangers to the pull of emotions, they too had feelings, and would welcome a warm, heartfelt blessing as much as any person would delight in a grandmother's hug. As an animal communicator, she could attest to that. Could it really be that over four decades had skipped by since one of the smallest creatures in the animal kingdom first spoke directly to her?

Bill and Margaret Edwards climbed the steps of All Souls Unitarian Church in New York City November 18, 2001, as was their custom every Sunday morning. Though what would follow later on in the afternoon at their church would not be so conventional. And that had both of them, as crusaders for the event, thrilled and a bit anxious. Not only would it be a first for the nearly 200-year-old church and its congregation, but it would also be especially so for the invited guests of honor, most who undoubtedly had never stepped beyond the sanctuary's threshold. Thank goodness, the smiling couple agreed in union, Sharon would be offering the homily at the Thanksgiving Blessing of the Animals, for the animals would feel at home with her.

As the afternoon special service neared, 14-year-old star athlete Jesse Mashburn stood at the church doors handing out programs for the blessings' service. How good was this, he thought, seeing people and their pets going to church together. Inside, his family and friends were stroking his animal companion to reassure the four-foot-long spotted ball python, aware that if the snake felt fear or tension, he'd ball up. But the reptile was content, wrapped around the arm of Jesse's sister. Jesse wondered if anyone else was sitting next to them. If so, not too close, he bet. Too bad some people don't understand that a snake is as true a friend as any dog or cat. And Willie was the sweetest animal he'd ever known.

Walking from her home just two blocks away from All Souls, church member Inez Miller escorted her best male friend, one who was half her age. Twenty-nine-year-old Petey preferred traveling with a soft cloth draped over his cage; the tropical Senegal parrot, with his gray head and tail, yellow vest and green body, was not a fan of wind, cool temperatures or too many people at once. As Jesse handed Mrs. Miller a program, she stepped inside and zeroed in on the first pew. Once seated, she let Petey out on her lap. Using some of his 50-word vocabulary, he talked freely, as he looked around, with quick head movements, at the new scenery, checking out where his human companion goes when she tells him she's going to church.

Second-grader Emily Donato had heard that a snake would be at the animal blessing today, so she decided not to bring her four rodent animal companions. Not that she didn't like all animals. She did help organize a local animal lovers' club and was a junior park ranger at Marine Park Environment Center. She considered it her mission in life to rescue as many animals as came across her path, from the sparrow she carried on her shoe after saving him from the street cleaner, to talking the pet shop owner into eliminating live white mice from the snakes' diets. But today she was going to be in charge of one of Bill Edwards' cats, Shakespeare, while Bill sang and helped with the blessing. Emily also wanted to see that lady, the one that talks to the animals. She wondered if she was like Dr. Doolittle, who could speak every animal's language.

Jumping out of the car with Annie secure in her canine carrier, Elizabeth Teal did a one-eighty, stuck her head back inside and thanked her friend for the lift. As she took the program from Jesse, Liz quickly ducked inside the church, and scoured the area for her husband and seven-year-old son. Finding them, she sat down with the 10-pound spaniel and a big sigh of relief. She'd made it. Earlier she'd been an hour and a half away in Rockland County at a meeting on training response dogs. An animal behavior specialist and trainer, Liz offered educational and emotional support for both ends of the leash. And for the past two months, stacking up hours upon hours at ground zero, where once the colossal World Trade Center dominated, she and Annie assisted other animal therapy teams who dealt with the aftermath of the disaster, knowing that the need to be touched and listened to is much more easily accepted when it's offered by an animal. Opening the program, Liz smiled when she read the name of the woman who would be giving the homily.

It'd been awhile since she'd first met the West Coast woman at a Delta Society meeting. Though the meeting had been succinct, she'd come away feeling that the petite, soft-spoken and unassuming woman cared deeply about animals and what messages they gave us about ourselves. So having Sharon Callahan, internationally acclaimed animal communicator and founder of Anaflora Flower Essence Therapy for Animals, a woman so many in animal care, from veterinarians to sanctuary providers to animal therapists respected, as the keynote speaker was apropos indeed as the church put on its first animal blessing.

Up in the choir loft, Bill Edwards surveyed the scene below. His gnawing concerns that this singular gathering of cats, hamsters, rabbits, mice, rats, dogs, bird and snake below in the pews would end up being as fragile as the glass animals in Tennessee Williams' play *The Glass Menagerie* were now thankfully shattered. Except for a couple of barks from two dogs in the back, the congregation of humans and animals seemed as peaceful and as natural a congregation as found at any Sunday service. His church's name—All Souls—seemed to be especially fitting for this inclusive gathering.

And more were still coming in for the blessing, including Margaret who'd returned home to bring 5 of the 40 cats who lived at her and her busband Bill's Feline Sanctuary, a loving shelter they had created for homeless cats. Handing the cats over to some children who didn't have animals of their own with them, including eight-year-old Emily, Margaret glanced up at Bill and gave him the thumbs up sign. For over a year, the couple had advocated a church recognition of the community's animal companions, from personal ones to those who serve as rescue and therapeutic animals. By June, All Souls got its ducks in a row and set on the November calendar A Thanksgiving Blessing of the Animals, not knowing then how relevant and healing the service would be once the events of September 11 etched their indelible mark on the city. With a wink and a smile, Bill nodded at Margaret, then turned to look at Mr. Socks, the animal companion of a close friend and fellow choir member, one of the few animals in the choir loft.

The big green-eyed and white-nosed tuxedo cat sat at the feet of Holly Drew. She was glad Mr. Socks was here. And he'd thrown her a perfect surprise: He'd settled in quite well as the choir practiced before the service, seemingly at home with the voices of so many humans in unison and the energy of so many other animals around him. Digging into her choir robe pocket, Holly felt for the picture of Woody. When she took Mr. Socks down to be blessed at the altar, she'd take the photo of her horse, a 17-year-old Morgan gelding, and his stable mate, Penney, who were five hours away at the family farm in Vermont. So bonded were the two horses that even Holly, an experienced equestrian who'd grown up with horses, was impressed with their intense attachment. She planned to show the photograph to Sharon Callahan, the woman who would be blessing Mr. Socks. Bill, who had utilized the services of the animal intuitive, as well as her flower essences for treating emotional imbalances in animals, spoke highly of this woman. Over and over he'd said her communication with his cats had resulted in authentic and compassionate help for the animals and him. But Holly was a natural skeptic and although she knew Sharon worked with vets and other animal care professionals around the country and the world, she would wait before casting her vote with Bill's.

With the last stragglers in, Jesse closed the doors and headed toward Willie. By the time he was settled and the brown-and-black-spotted ball python was at ease draped around his neck, the service in the white interior of the classical revival church was already moving along. Looking around the auditorium, he liked the idea of this whole thing. It was a cool way for people to come together and show what they had in common: their love for their animal companions. The way Jesse looked at it, when people treated animals nicely, they treated people nicely, too. And with so many people he knew still stressed out about 9/11, that was a good thing. At the podium, a diminutive woman rose to speak. This was the animal intuitive he'd heard about. As he petted Willie, he gave Sharon Callahan his full attention.

Moved by the beauty of the scene before her, Sharon looked out at the sanctuary with moist eyes. As a child, this is how she'd envisioned church: a beautiful, spiritual place where all God's creatures joined together. The congregation, dotted with home-based and serviced-based animals, along with their human companions, emitted the high vibration of oneness and love. Thanking God for the peace she felt in church again, Sharon also thanked the Universe for this harmonious place, where humans and animals treated one another with sacred respect and love.

Though her focus was on her presentation and not on communicating with the individual animals, a few had dropped in to speak. The snake said he was so proud to be here and liked being touched by everyone; he felt he was performing a sacred service to his species in showing people snakes don't feel icky and that they are as loving as any animal. Annie the dog, a veteran of animal-assisted therapy, threw in a reminder to not forget those animals out there helping people in crisis situations. Jumping from his human companion's lap to the woman's shoulder, a spirited parrot relayed to her that he was thinking of calling out "here kitty" like he does at home, but he figured he'd keep the feline teasing down to a minimum. He was having fun just being with everyone and showing off his handsome feathers anyway. She chuckled at that one. Just as with humans, there was always a comedian in the place.

Before Sharon spoke, she noticed a young girl holding and stroking a cat from head to tail. The cat's delight reminded her not only of the smiling Cheshire cat in Alice in Wonderland, but also of Lily, her own feline buddy back at home. Smiling, Sharon began the homily.

"When we think of service animals, we often think of guide dogs, search and rescue dogs and other animals that are trained to assist human beings, but it is my feeling that all animals perform tremendous acts of service. I believe that animals are here on earth as a sacred ministry. According to *Webster's Dictionary*, to minister means to offer comfort, to aid and to tend to the needs of others. To any sensitive person, the ministry of domestic animals can be observed in the ways in which their lives complement and support our own. In addition to functioning as our companions and protectors, domestic animals live as examples of universal virtues that we seek to perfect within ourselves: beauty, humility, sacrifice, service, devotion, patience and unconditional love, just to name a few. Wild animals, simply by virtue of their presence in the world, have the ability to uplift and transform the human spirit, thus being service to the blossoming of the human soul. . . . Animals also serve one another."

Offering examples of animal altruism and love, Sharon delivered authentic stories that had ears of all shapes listening. Some in the audience even offered an amen, as more than once her words were underscored by a canine bark.

With her picture of Woody and Penney in hand and Mr. Socks in tow, Holly led the procession down to the altar where Sharon, along with Bill, the Reverends Forrester Church and Jan Carlson-Bull, stood ready to pay tribute to the individual animals. When Holly neared Sharon, she felt a big presence from this tiny, alabaster-skinned woman whose eyes sparkled with gentle compassion. As Sharon took the photograph of the two horses and focused on the images, she seemed to forget her surroundings for a millisecond and gently merged with the animals facing her in the picture. Looking up from the photo at Holly, she stated with a Mona Lisa smile, "Oh, my, they really, truly love each other, don't they? How wonderful."

Taken aback and greatly moved that this woman picked up something so fundamental about Woody and Penney, Holly almost forgot to present Mr. Socks. As she did, Sharon touched the cat and offered a blessing for all four of them. Aware of the many behind her, Holly scooted away knowing that she had been blessed in more ways than one.

Liz with Annie, Emily with Shakespeare, Jesse with Willie and Inez, accompanying Petey, made their way down the aisle to the front of the church. Like the others, they came forward with their animal companions to receive blessings for a life full of joy, appreciation and love.

Still swathed in the electric, yet soothing energy she felt being around Sharon, Holly loaded Mr. Socks in the cab. Calm and content, the cat had experienced his first church service, his first blessing. Holly was eager to be with Woody to see how he and Penny were after receiving their blessings from this spiritually intuitive woman. As the cab slipped into traffic, Holly knew she wanted to know more. Just who *was* this singular being? What messages from our animal partners did she have for us all?

Sharon Callahan and puppy Isabella communicate.

2

A CHILD PAYS ATTENTION

Children pay better attention than grownups.
If Fern says that the animals in Zuckerman's
barn talk, I'm quite ready to believe her.
Perhaps if people talked less, animals would
talk more. People are incessant talkers—I
can give you my word on that.

Charlotte's Web, E.B. White

oving gently to the ground, the curly-haired five-year-old positioned herself on her hands and knees. She wanted to be on the same level as her cat, who was locked into a steadfast stare with something he had cornered in the backyard. Sharon's gentle gray eyes followed his gaze and came eye to eye with a tiny creature that looked like a space alien, just like the drawing she'd seen in her father's morning newspaper.

She had brought salamanders, along with their dirt habitat, into the bathtub: She had rolled in the grass with their dog, provided a secure lap for a rabbit, offered a finger perch to the bird, an open room for white mice and a shared bed for the cat, but never had she come in contact with, well, such a scary-looking bug.

Yet, it was the insect who seemed terrified of the cat, a feline who obviously was not swayed by the praying mantis' efforts to stand her ground. Continuing to wave her arms to fend off the cat, she suddenly turned toward the little girl. At that moment, Sharon felt herself merging with the tiny animal; she sensed her inner fear, saw mental pictures of little praying mantises and, through thought transfer, heard her plead quite clearly, "Please don't let the cat hurt me. I have a family, and I shouldn't die now."

Though she had always felt tied to animals, as tied as those big knots she'd seen securing the boats in the nearby San Francisco Bay, she'd never had one speak directly to her. Yet she didn't feel concerned about this turn of events; it seemed quite natural to merge with this tiny animal.

Her only conundrum right now was how to deal with this creature's plea. Having never missed a meal, the cat was too strong for the tiny girl, who, as her mother and father noted over and over, was petite for a kindergartener. She couldn't remove him from the standoff. And he was quick. One paw could swat and cut her in a flash.

Screwing her courage to the sticking place, Sharon picked up the praying mantis and placed her in a willow tree. In the afternoon heat, the two looked at one another for several minutes. Breaking the exchange, the praying mantis went up a branch, turning around midway to say, "Thank you very much. Sometime in the future I'll return the favor. I'll show up when you need proof that you are following your heart's lead. Just watch for me. Good day."

Through the kitchen window, her mother, Virginia, looked at her daughter—always the loner, with no interest in playing with other children. And so shy and quiet, silent past the age most kids speak. Frightened of people, yet her eldest seemed so unafraid of what she might find in nature, where the raven-haired Irish-American was completely at ease. Her love for animals went beyond most children's attachment to their pets and included all animals no matter the species or the personality. What was she rescuing today?

Swinging her black patent leather Sunday shoes back and forth, nine-year-old Sharon looked down the pew at her parents and two sisters, four-year-old Molly and two-year-old Sally, then scanned the church. She liked the feeling of the space: tall ceilings, the saints holding their vigils along the sides of the pews, the candles burning for loved ones. But she would like the church even better if animals could help fill the pews. Everything would seem more natural then. But, after what she'd heard in catechism class a few days ago, she guessed that wouldn't happen any time soon.

The after-school religious study class was in a building attached to the church. Here the priest would instruct the children in the ways of the Catholic religion. On this day, he was talking about God's creation. He spoke about mankind. He then turned to the lower creatures of the planet, those God had not made in his image. Soul-less, all animals were sent here only to be employed by God's children, the humans on the earth, he said. Like the slash of a knife, the priest's words cut through Sharon's heart. Gasping, Sharon covered her mouth with her hand. But she could not cover up her disbelief at the cleric's statements, nor the inner anger and deep sadness she felt. Didn't he know that all God's creatures had feelings and thoughts and could express them as much as any of us? Crossing her arms, Sharon vowed never to trust this church stuff again.

And today, she would keep her promise, only relenting to listen if the priest would talk today about one of the saints she'd been reading about. She crossed her fingers that St. Francis would be his topic. That guy was neat. Like her, he not only loved animals, he empathized with them. And like her, he led a solitary life. She understood that, for she too preferred being alone, alone with her animal friends, that is. Not that she didn't love her family, but her raison d'etre was intertwined with those who spoke not only sparingly, but from the heart, without concern for what someone else would think.

Upstairs in her room, Sharon played with her toy horses. But her mind was on yesterday when her grandfather had taught Molly and her a lesson about animals. Grandfather Oscar, a world traveler who sought to see animals in their native habitats and not in zoos, was sad when the two brought home a pair of eggs from a robin's nest. In their excitement to hatch the eggs under a light and to raise chicks, they had forgotten the mother, who, their grandfather said, would mourn when she returned to the nest to find her unhatched babies missing. He pointed out that each animal has his way of life and purpose and that no one should interfere with that. As Sharon returned the eggs to their nest, she felt the grieving mother nearby. That experience would stay with her forever.

Another lesson wasn't far behind. At her grandfather's 19th-century farmhouse in Stockton, he had one cat that would go out in the yard, grab a chicken and drag her through the cat door into the kitchen. Distressed, the chicken showered the room with her feathers, while Sharon's grandmother Peggy, claiming domain in her kitchen, tried to nudge the chicken out with a broom.

Disturbed by the commotion and the chicken's anxiety, Sharon decided to speak to the cat. Explaining she was upset and he shouldn't hurt the chicken, the cat responded that he was not hurting the chicken, and he had no intention of stopping his game. He was teaching the chicken something—she should get over being scared and learn it was only about having fun. Whether he intended to or not, the cat also supplied Sharon with two animal tutorials from the Universe: animals not only have their purposes, but also their own perceptions of any event. And they have free will, as humans do, about whether to communicate with another being and whether to agree to another's requests, even a caring human being who has a talent for talking with animals.

School was not a favorite place for the shy 12-year-old, who brought no one home from the all-girls parochial school to befriend. Classes were not interesting, though reading was one of Sharon's favorite pastimes. Her bookshelves attested to that. On her bedside table, one book kept a comforting vigil among the toy animals. It was the best book she'd ever read and read and read. She'd lost count of how many times she'd devoured the 184 pages of *Charlotte's Web*. It'd made perfect sense that Fern could talk with Charlotte the spider, Wilbur the pig and all the barnyard animals. One of her favorite parts was Dr. Dorian's reply to Fern's mother when she asked if he believed Fern could talk to the animals: "If Fern says the animals in Zuckerman's barn talk, I'm quite ready to believe her. Perhaps if people talked less, animals would talk more. People are incessant talkers—I can give you my word on that."

A non-talker herself, Sharon always chuckled at the doctor's wise words. She wished she knew a Dr. Dorian. Maybe he could reassure her parents. Aware that they often worried about their taciturn daughter and her fondness for isolating herself in her room, Sharon would want the doctor to explain that she, like Fern, was a listener first and a talker second.

Sharon also appreciated the friendship Charlotte the barn spider and Wilbur the pig had in *Charlotte's Web*, and the way they helped each other: Charlotte writing the life-saving "some pig" in her web to save

Wilbur's life and he in turn helping her young ones survive. Nothing was more important than listening and helping when asked.

Only last week, a neighbor had brought her dog to see the girl who had a way with animals. The accident-prone boxer had been hit by a car three times and would have fits of chasing his tail in circles. When Sharon tuned in to the dog, she was shown images of mistreatment in this lifetime before he'd come to live with the woman and lifetimes before that. Having been beaten, drowned, thrown off high places and shot, he had begun to believe this would always been his fate and that he must deserve to be not only hurt, but fatally so. Aware that most troubled animals, like people in therapy, need to tell their story to start their healing inside, she bore witness to his experiences, choices and karmic patterns.

By merging with the dog, feeling what he was feeling, she tuned in to his frequency and received the feeling-pictures of his life story he was sending her. When he finished, she passed no judgment or analysis, but with great compassion, suggested he let go of his old beliefs and cycles and choose to accept the joy that life was offering him now. Sharon then turned to the woman and broke the silence by telling her she thought the dog would be better now. She didn't explain how and why, nor did the woman ask. But the dog no longer had any painful mishaps. After that, other people in the community with sick or troubled animals began to drop by when they saw Sharon outside in the yard, though she rarely shared that with her family.

Not that Sharon's family would have been surprised at her intuitive abilities with animals; they had seen her bring home countless needy animals, and the family had its own beloved collection. Nor would they have been surprised to learn that she had not revealed this gift to them. That was Sharon, ever the solitary, silent one.

Extremely quiet and sensitive was how Sharon's mom would describe her oldest child. Sensitive to the way people talked to her, and sensitive to cruelty of any kind, especially when it came to animals. More than once, she and her husband had talked about their diffident daughter's unique preference for the company of animals over her peers.

Sharing a room, the two younger girls felt that Sharon was someone they didn't know at all. Sally, seven years younger, felt that her oldest sister was closed off, and she often interpreted this buffer as selfishness. Molly, closer in age to Sharon, could depend on her sister to laugh with her at times. But she also knew she was extremely introspective and preferred seclusion in her bedroom. Yet, she had also seen Sharon in her element. While she and Sally played stickball with local kids, Sharon, a hard-core tomboy, would often desert the game for any animal in the neighborhood who she felt was being ignored or hurt. Animals gravitated around Sharon anyway. If one of her rescued animals or one of the family ones died, she would always hold a sacred ceremony to honor their lives and their passing. Her uncanny bond with animals was just who she was.

For Molly, one incident would forever stand out as a testament to that. As she and Sharon were occupied at the bottom of the stairs, they looked up to see the family cat coming down the stairs with Ratty, Sharon's white rat, in his mouth. With an unwavering calmness, Sharon talked to the feline as he tiptoed down the stairs. Ratty did not move, seemingly not so much from fear, but from trust, as if he were aware Sharon was orchestrating the event. Focused on the soft-spoken girl, the cat treaded tenderly toward her, where Sharon waited with an outstretched hand. Once there, he dropped his potential dinner in her hand and walked away.

PERUSHA ANANDA

Even as a little girl, Sharon connected with cats in a singular, insightful way.

3

SECRETS AND SECLUSION

I like to have humans talk to me. Mr. Morris

often reads his sermons to me, and Miss

Laura tells me secrets that I don't think

she'd tell to anyone else.

Beautiful Joe, Marshall Saunders

As a teenager in the early 1960s, Sharon grew even more solitary. Outside in nature, she could entertain herself for hours with a spider, a frog or a worm, observing their routines. By merging with them, she picked up their feeling-images and talked with them. But she'd long ago learned most people didn't see or feel life that way. She just knew that, other than the reliable companionship of Mother Nature, she felt as if she didn't belong here, and that somehow she'd simply been dropped off on the wrong planet.

That belief never seemed more raw than when talk about her future spearheaded the family conversation. Though her parents never discouraged her from her steadfast curiosity about critters, they often reminded her she eventually had to put that aside and make some plans for earning a living. When she said she would be a veterinarian, they asked how that could be when not only had she repeatedly announced she didn't want to go to college, but, as her grades verified, she was also not college-prep material. Though she scored high on comprehension tests, she had a propensity for getting mixed up when it came to math and writing. In those days, no one had yet heard of dyslexia. Bright kids like Sharon, who transposed numbers and letters and learned in a different way, were considered unmotivated students, not working up to their potential. True talents, often artistic or esoteric, went unnoticed.

For the sensitive teen, the academic frustration only compounded her notion about school: It was dullsville, and compared to what the animals had to teach her, it was double dullsville. She could listen to the creatures talk nonstop. But what Sharon didn't like to hear was unnecessary talk, people chatter, whether from adults or people her age. It didn't interest her, just as the school social scene didn't interest her. She never dated and only once did she attend an extracurricular event, a high school ball. The affair only emphasized her feelings of being a misfit, an alien on a stopover on planet earth.

She knew that exasperated her parents, especially her dad. A college-educated and successful businessman, Frank Callahan provided his family with an upper-middle-class lifestyle and had shown that he could be a family man, loving and giving. He had a gun collection, but, with his love for animals, refused to hunt; instead, he taught his girls target shooting.

Yet it was his politics that his daughter most admired. A free thinker, he left the Republican Party for the Democrats to become heavily involved with the civil rights movement. But his strong anti-discrimination beliefs didn't fit in with the conservative climate of his professional life, and it took its toll. But that wasn't all. Though he had been prescribed medication for manic depression, alcohol would often become his solace, to the detriment of his personal relationships. More and more, the drinking etched a granite wall between Sharon's parents. After the girls were kissed, put to bed and their doors closed, late night arguments would sometimes erupt. Sharp words of frustration and disappointment ricocheted off the walls. Soon her disillusioned dad and mom became more distant from each other.

Saddened that her parents seemed to be missing the simple joys of life, she wanted to tell them to look around at the natural world. Could they not see that all things, even rocks, were not only sacred, but were alive with vibrations that could hoist one's spirits higher than any of those space rockets the whole country seemed so excited about?

Books also lifted her spirits. *Charlotte's Web* still claimed a secure spot in her heart, but a second book was now homesteading her nightstand, stirring up emotions as grand as the Golden Gate Bridge. Inspired by its simplicity and wisdom, Sharon felt a passionate kinship with *Beautiful Joe,* the autobiography of a dog who tells his life story with the help of a woman friend. Published in the late 19th century in Canada, it was the first book to sell a million copies. But more importantly, *Beautiful Joe* sparked a movement to treat animals more humanely.

Based on a true story, the chronicle features a dog whose abusive owner savagely chops off his ears and tail in a fit of anger. But the dog is saved by a passing boy who takes the ailing dog home to his caring family, including a sister, Laura. It is she who names the physically marred dog Beautiful Joe. Their rapport, along with Beautiful Joe's many observations about animals, their feelings and relationships with people, fills the moving autobiography. It was unlike any book Sharon had read before.

Beautiful Joe also inspired her to continue using her ability to communicate with animals, as if she could stop anyway. It was just a part of her, a gift that she didn't question. And though she'd been told more than once "you can't just spend your life hanging out with animals," she knew that one day she'd use this skill to speak for the animals, to help them communicate with their human companions. She didn't know how, but she just knew it.

Beautiful Joe became even more real to Sharon when the family made a trip to Lake Tahoe. Staying in the small town of Bijou, they spotted more than once a wiry black-haired dog outside their motel. Realizing that orphan dogs often ended up being shot to keep down their population, Sharon convinced her parents to let "the ugliest, most beautiful poodle-terrier" fly home with them. Joining the animal household, Bijou, so named for the canine's hometown by her dad, soon became an integral part of the family makeup.

But Bijou's relationship with Sharon went beyond that; they were not only buddies who played *chase-slide* across the slippery house floors, they were souls who communicated openly. They were like Laura and Joe in *Beautiful Joe*: "I like to have humans talk to me. Mr. Morris often reads his sermons to me, and Miss Laura tells me secrets that I don't think she'd tell anyone else."

Besides the feeling pictures Bijou would send to Sharon, Bijou had a rubber face capable of conveying a distinct range of expressions, from humor to disgust, complete with rolling eyes. Though his early life taught him that life could be serious and ephemeral, Bijou could clown around, reminding her that life was about fun. Unlike Sharon, he was gregarious and had a knack for knowing where the party was. Maybe in his own way, she would sometimes think, he was mirroring something to her about her life.

There were other animals around with whom Sharon connected. As a teen, though she'd long ended her play sessions with her toy horses, horses still held a place in Sharon's heart. Just looking at a picture of a horse could give her the same feeling that most girls her age had when they saw a photo of Paul McCartney or some other rock star who made them shiver. Except horses for Sharon, and probably most female equestrians, represented that virile male energy that was safe while also spirited.

Well, *some* were spirited; but, unfortunately, not the ones she'd come to know lately. Her parents had set up riding lessons for her, but she found the horses so unhappy with their unchallenging, joyless routine and cloistered environment, she could not bear their sadness and let go of the reins for good.

And meeting Blackie only augmented her decision. In a pasture near her home, a swayback horse, who had spent his life walking in circles turning a mill wheel, caught her eye. She stopped and watched as the elderly black horse grazed in a perfect circle, unable to move in any other fashion. Pictures of Blackie working 12-hour days harnessed to a wheel rushed into her mind's eye. Aware of the work animals do for people, some of it harsh, she became intensely sad. Blackie broke in with his own story. Yes, he'd worked long hours and he was incredibly worn down, but he'd believed that was his job; that was all he had ever known. What he didn't understand was why so much had been expected of him. He had wanted to serve, but in giving service, had yearned to be treated with basic respect and kindness. Yet, just as he'd never complained during his grueling work hours, he wasn't sad about it now. He was just very worn out. Maybe one day she could tell people about the importance of caring for service animals. She said she would.

Back at home, cats remained an integral part of Sharon's life. Padding around the family home, the house was the cats' domain. With their lithe, yet strong, sensuous bodies, coupled with an otherworldly perspective on living in the here and now, cats often were the more mystical of those she communicated with. And any story with felines in it always roused her attention.

Not long ago, she'd read a book on the life of St. Julian of Norwich, who spent her life in a room with a walled garden off the church; her only companion was her cat. The only time she had to deal with people was when the town folk would come to the small window in the wall to tell her their problems. St. Julian liked being of service, but she valued her untamed relationship with the Divine and nature even more. That sense of wildness seemed to be a thread within all the stories she read about the mystics, as well as something even more germane: they all had visions, just as she had had and still did. But most of all, they always seemed attached to animals.

While in her teens, Sharon ran across the writings of Dr. Edward Bach, an English physician of the early 20th century who specialized in bacteriology and immunology. His 60-page *Heal Thyself—An Explanation of the Real Cause and Cure of Disease* spoke to her much the same way the animals did; it seemed to make perfect sense. She scoured the library for more information about this cool doctor who ventured outside his training in conventional medicine in his quest for a down-to-earth, natural way to treat his patients.

Sharon discovered the innovative physician turned first to homeopathy and then to developing his own system of healing. Noting that emotional/spiritual imbalances, such as fear and negativity, could not only erode the physical body, but also create a fertile ground for illness, Bach shifted his attention to the healing vibrations of flowers. His method, though powerful, was seemingly simple. On the surface of a bowl of spring water, a flower was placed in the sunlight for several hours, charging the water with an energetic imprint of the flower's vibrational signature. With these tinctures and a treatment plan using particular flowers to treat certain imbalances, he helped many people. His energetic medicine became known as Bach Flowers.

When she got out of high school, Sharon worked in an insurance office in San Francisco and attended the College of Marin. In an art class, she met Bill, her first male friend. The two decided to marry when, after their first and only sexual encounter, Sharon became pregnant. Never really lovers or in love, the union lasted only a few months following daughter Jennifer's birth. She didn't want to return to her parents' home, so to pay the rent on the small apartment, Sharon began work as a waitress.

Nearly two years later, a second fissure surfaced in her life. Her father, who had quit drinking, but who had also stopped taking his prescribed lithium, took a gun from his prized collection and fatally shot himself. Like her mother and sisters, she was shattered. She took Bijou to live with Jennifer and her for the next decade. Always a comfort and a confidant to both of them, the dog was the cornerstone to their family unit.

Though Sharon still communicated with animals, mostly at the requests of friends and neighbors, her focus was now on her daughter, and for the next 12 years she supported her on her own. It was not easy, financially or emotionally. The ebony-haired, blue-eyed China doll was normal, but found to be low functioning. Jennifer's friendly persona earned her the title of 'the little girl who never met a stranger.' But with Sharon's persistent efforts to get a good education for her, Jennifer received a novelty at the time—a state-funded voucher to attend a private school. Sharon became an advocate for children with learning problems, setting up an organization in Marin County for children with learning disabilities.

David came into the restaurant where Sharon worked and into her life when Jennifer was 11. After they married in 1979, the family moved to Mt. Shasta, a town in the shadow of the majestic mountain blessed with a bounty of seasonal wildflowers. Never had she seen such radiant and colorful flora! Over time she gobbled up books and gained information about the local plants, but it wasn't until she met 80-year-old native Edward Stool, an expert in the field, that she could identify the Mt. Shasta flowers as easily as those in her own garden. And until his death, he was her mentor and her friend.

She still occasionally responded when friends asked her for insight to their animals, but her primary focus was meeting the demands of the dutiful wife, hosting dinners and staying involved with local society. Slowly, however, she began to feel disconnected to her lifestyle and her husband. Never an angry person, she expressed her unhappiness with acute sadness. And once Jennifer was out of the house and on her own, the feeling that something was missing in her life only intensified. Soon depression crept in and, for a while, even agoraphobia. Sharon tried to ignore the feelings, but finally in 1987, stuffing a few clothes and cat Haiku in a backpack, she walked away from the fine house, nice furniture, cars and bank accounts and never returned. Two miles away, she stopped at a coffeehouse and began talking to an elderly hippie woman she'd seen around town before. For the next year, she stayed with her and began working at a doctor's office, never taking one penny from David then or when the divorce was final two years later.

As she managed psychiatrist Tom Seeley's office for the next four years, she also found herself helping more people with their animal concerns. She began to feel alive again in spirit, but not in her physical body. She could work only when she was well enough. Her supportive boss let her do some work at home. Coming in waves, flu-like symptoms would engulf her. Medical tests revealed nothing.

As she became more debilitated from the mysterious ailment, something else hit her to the core of her being. Her beautiful and happy daughter, now living with her fiancé, vanished. Leaving without her personal belongings or any clues to her disappearance, 25-year-old Jennifer was gone.

Merging with dogs and other animals, Sharon found that their thoughts interested her more than the chattering of people.

After two years of intensive police work, with no trace of the friendly, young woman so well liked in the community, officials closed the case, marking it unsolved. Sharon marked it devastating. Through the months of searching for Jennifer on her own, with time bringing only faded hope, she felt the ache in her heart pound like a big bass drum. But nothing could prepare her for the gut-wrenching grief that now permeated her life. Longing for the touch of her daughter's hand, she felt the grieving would never abate. It was during these hollow days that her illness took a left turn, diving into an abyss of mentally and physically incapacitating fog. But the clouds were broken by an experience that would not only transform her, but light her way back home to her own inner truth and passion.

4

THE RECONNECTION

*How it is that animals understand things, I do
not know, but it is certain that they do
understand. Perhaps there is a language which
is not made of words and everything in the
world understands it. Perhaps there is a soul
hidden in everything and it can always speak,
without even making a sound, to another soul.*

A Little Princess, Frances Hodgson Burnett

In and out of the hospital like a yo-yo, Sharon felt decades older than her 42 years. After innumerable medical tests, the mystery ailment remained just that. Vowing she would undergo no more futile exams and tests, she locked herself in her apartment, determined to get well or get on the last train out of this life. At her side, companions Lily, a gold-streaked gray tabby, and Shoji, a small gray mixed breed, continued their steadfast vigil. Friends, concerned for her welfare, left food and encouraging words outside Sharon's door.

One night, as a high fever simmered throughout her body, she lay on the bed, dizzy with an intense chest pain. Feeling disconnected, she felt her spirit separate from her body and float upward. From the ceiling, she noticed below a motionless woman drenched in agony on a bed. Poor thing; she looks so wretched. The compassion transformed to astonishment: she was that woman!

Turning away to look up, Sharon realized the ceiling was not only ascending higher and higher, but within its center, was a round hole that opened to the night. Drawn to the aperture, she was gently pulled through a luminous, transparent tube that reached far into space. Inside the warm and bright cylinder, she was soothed by music both glorious and unearthly.

How strange, she thought, I have no body, yet I can sense so much. Headed toward a bright, pulsating light that vibrated with the rhythm of a heartbeat, she butted up against what appeared to be a rubbery, thin, invisible membrane, and after three strikes—is there stickball here, she wondered—she popped out. There were no people to greet her, but the beauty and peace of the place spoke its own language.

Around her, a pristine alpine meadow alive with wildflowers, tall trees, rocks, insects and animals of every kind in a composite of all the various natural earth habitats—desert, forest, sea, island, ice field. Throughout her bodyless self, she could sense the intenseness of the environment—the smells, sounds, even warmth and sight. She needed only to focus her awareness on something and she could see it both myopically and from a far distance. But what really jolted her was the aliveness of her thoughts, how her consciousness could make even the substance of the ether move. Why, with all this vibrancy and serenity, she observed, surely this is heaven.

"No, you are not in heaven. You can't go that far. This is the place where the blueprints are kept, and you are here to look at your blueprint," the animals communicated telepathically.

"Blueprint?" Sharon asked.

A large deer with magnificent antlers approached her:

> "All beings, whether human or animal, take a body on the earth plane, create a blueprint before incarnation. Drawn with help from one's Divine source, guardian angels and guides, the plan is for the perfect unfolding of the highest good for the individual. With human beings, much of the blueprint is forgotten after childhood. By adulthood, a mere ghost image remains, just enough to cause the soul a slight restlessness when it's out of alignment with the original blueprint.

"Animals are in charge of the blueprints, both here and on earth. Each animal species is consecrated for its purpose, and each individual animal is anointed as well. Some beings, such as the great whales and the elephants, are record keepers. They record within their being the entire history of earth and each creature upon her.

"Now, in relationship to human beings, a soul that has taken the form of an animal companion has recall not only of its own blueprint, but the divine blueprint of its human companion. Aware of the entire karmic pattern, the animal holds the vibration of the human in its exalted state and does everything in his power to direct the human toward harmony with the original blueprint. Not a small task, you see. Every animal on earth is doing this job. Are you ready to look at your blueprint?"

Gathering around her, the animals offered strength and compassion as Sharon stepped into a holographic review of her life. In visual and emotional detail, the movie flashed before her not only of every scene she had experienced in her life, but how every action or inaction had affected herself and others. She felt her pain and their pain. It was not that she had done terrible things, but that she'd often left things unsaid and undone: feelings of love and encouragement she had not expressed to others, and moments when she could have been helpful and wasn't. With this open perspective, she also saw how actions she thought of as normal and insignificant at the time, like making eye contact with an animal on a certain day, were just the opposite. They had brought encouragement and compassion. But the most recurring story line was when she had strayed from her blueprint and had turned her back on her life's work.

Leaving the movie of her past, she was guided into a second holographic image of her own divine blueprint. Within the matrix, she saw her entire life as she had laid it out for herself before being born. Fueled by a profound feeling of attunement, she was showered by a loving light, a Grace that aligned with her soul. She saw how life on earth could be if she'd surrender to the Divine Expression within her, that Christ consciousness which connected her to all things. The ego self, so prominent in humans, was to stand second in line to the spirit self, which has the compassion and courage to use one's unique gifts without fear. As a sense of bliss enveloped Sharon, she felt surrender, purpose and universal harmony simultaneously.

The animals again spoke:

> "This is who you really are. We have offered this vibration for you to summon when you get off track; you can recall this memory by simply remembering this feeling. You will need it, for the energy on your planet, with its many distractions, can become very dense.

> "The next hologram is about your future. Remember, your blueprint is a plan that outlines what you aim to experience to grow as spirit. As all beings have free will, or choice, how you do that, how you fill it in, is up to you. It is like giving a child crayons and a coloring book. How the child colors the outlined figures in the book is up to the child. There are no wrong colors, but there are some colors that can make the pictures more easily resonate like a brilliant piece of art."

Before her, many images flickered brightly: scenes of events, people and animals that would appear in her life if she so chose. Two in particular struck a melodious chord. The first illustration proffered two men sitting in a sunny field, one with long, flowing white hair, but it was the second image that stirred up a sense of intense urgency. Rooted in her love of animals and flowers, the picture showed her connecting with the plants and creating a system of healing. Picking flowers, she would place them in bowls of water and later pour the liquid into bottles that had healing names, such as Return to Joy.

Over and over again, the animals communicated to her the importance of all blueprints. Though animals have group souls, each is unique with its own purpose and blueprint to experience, whether alone or through their relationships with human companions. As partners with people, the animals have not only an opportunity to play out their blueprints, but also a duty to assist humans with their divine blueprints. As guardians of their human companions' spiritual plan, animals are acutely aware of the magnitude and the honor of this sacred arrangement.

As she moved out of that hologram, the animal-peppered meadow engulfed her again. Before she left them, the animals asked that she do some things upon her return to life in her physical body. Some were simple. Cats, whether big and wild or house cats, asked that she convey to people to please not keep them indoors against their will if at all possible. Part of the reason they are on earth is to work with the planet's energy, and they can only do that if they are able to put their feet on the ground.

Other requests would be made. These important messages would come to her as she began to work with animals and their human companions back on the physical plane. "But now," the animals said, "it is time for you to go back to begin the task that was long ago forgotten. We will help you. The animals do not forget that they have come to earth to be of service. Human beings, on the other hand, as they take on a physical body, almost always do. We will remain deeply connected, and through our kind back on your planet, messages of Universal Truth will ring out. You need only listen."

Chilly from the evaporating sweat on her skin, Sharon pulled the covers up to her chin. Still foggy, and feeling the familiar aches of her illness returning, she slowly looked around her bedroom. She hadn't died after all, but the near death experience (NDE) had made its alterations. Starting with her vision. All that lay before her shimmered with light, its basic component. Living and nonliving had no distinction; all vibrated with light. In seeing energy visually, she could also see the spaces between the molecules that formed objects. But it was the sparkles that intrigued her, for she had seen the world this way before. As a child, before she started school, she had seen the sparkling glow around people and animals.

She reached out for Lily and Shoji, ever her constant companions. With purrs and heads bowed for stroking, the luminous felines confirmed that they, using their intuitive skills, had been reliable witnesses to the experience. They would nudge her memory when needed. She hugged them, rose from the bed, and headed for the front door. She opened it wide and told them they could go out. Afraid that the traffic on the busy street would be deadly, she had forbidden the cats from going outdoors previously. Blasé Lily, once a feral cat, padded out to reclaim nature's landscape. But Shoji, having never been outside, gingerly walked on the grass, then scooted up a nearby tree. In sync with the little feline's movements, Sharon felt his sensation of paws on velvet grass and claws gripping the coarse tree bark as he ascended to the first limb. Mystically in step with his emotions, she felt his sheer delight; and more than that, her own. No more locked doors for her two companions.

Other lifestyle changes tiptoed into her thoughts, though it would be awhile before all the events and knowledge from the NDE would surface. Though still drained and shaky, she felt a resurgence for life, a joie de vivre that made her simply want to smile and just be. And the world looked different to her.

The ring of the phone jerked her back to the demands of the everyday world. Answering, she heard the voice of her old boss and physician friend. He'd run across some information that he believed would help her: Would she have her doctor test her for a new disease that was just beginning to surface? It was called Lyme disease.

PERUSHA ANANDA

Cats asked Sharon to convey to people that they be allowed, if at all possible, to go outdoors to work with the earth's energy (Lily and Shoji).

5

FLOWER POWER

*"O Tiger-lily," said Alice, addressing herself to
one that was waving gracefully about in the
wind, "I wish you could talk!"*

*"We can talk," said the Tiger-lily, "when
there's somebody worth talking to."*

Through the Looking Glass, Lewis Carroll

*T*he big-brimmed straw hat and the long-sleeved purple shirt protected Sharon's fair skin from the early morning sun. Since the NDE, her sensitivity to light had increased. On her arm, a wicker basket containing crystal bowls and a jug of spring water swayed to the rhythm of her steps. Suddenly, she stopped in a small glen, put down her basket and did a 360, emulating a playful Maria in *The Sound of Music*. Before her, wildflowers dotted the base of Mt. Shasta, popping up along the hillsides, stream banks, ridges and crannies of the sacred mountain.

Like a Duke Ellington jazz composition, their vibrations stimulated and soothed; like a Winslow Homer painting, their colors reached out and grabbed the eye, as their perfumes fluttered in the air. With their signature vibrations, the flowers also communicated a compelling earth language. But, thought Sharon, their biggest asset was their indigenous healing power: Shooting Star, an orange celestial-shaped delight, replaces feelings of alienation with a sense of belonging; iris, with regal flags of blue-violet, encourages playfulness and is good for animals confined to artificial environments; Castle Lake azalea, the beauty-in-adversity pink delicacy with its long-tongued stamens, relieves the effects of abuse, abandonment and unkindness; and, one of her personal favorites, Tiger lily, the freckle-faced orange flower, fosters peaceful cooperation with other animals and humans.

Tiger lily always shifted her back to her childhood and her cherished book *Through the Looking Glass*. She recited the familiar passage: "O Tiger-lily," said Alice, addressing herself to one that was waving gracefully about in the wind, "I *wish* you could talk!" "We can talk," said the Tiger-lily, "when there's somebody worth talking to."

Laughing, Sharon thought, well, I hope I'm worth talking to today. It'd be an honor, as always. Lowering herself to the ground, Sharon crossed her legs and sat in her customary reflective pose. Before she began her spiritual contemplation, she reflected on the changes in her life over the past two years: the life-altering NDE; the Lyme disease diagnosis and subsequent low-dose antibiotic treatment; the slow, steady mending of a broken heart over the disappearance of her beloved Jennifer; gratis room and board at the Josephine Taylor Foundation, where subtle energy research was ongoing; her continued communication with animals and now this—creating flower essences to treat animals, just as the NDE had shown her.

Leaving mundane thoughts behind, she merged with the surrounding floral landscape and soon melded with the flowers. During the spiritual communion, the flowers instructed her on their individual healing properties and how a particular essence can address physical, mental or emotional/spiritual imbalances. As the schematics concluded, she respectfully requested permission to retrieve a bit of each flower to make energetic medicine; she also asked that the meadow's guardian angels and nature spirits bless the process.

Gently removing just enough from each flower to cover the water's surface in the crystal bowl, she placed the blossoms in the glass containers. Setting each bowl in the sunlight adjacent to their paternal plants, Sharon offered prayers that the blossoms transfer their electromagnetic energies to the water to aid in the healing of animals and animal-human relationships. She thanked them for keeping animals attuned to nature and their natural connection to the Universe.

For the next three hours, as the solar light passed through the flowers and nature formulated its elixirs, Sharon retreated to her books: *Vibrational Medicine* by Dr. Richard Gerber, *The Living Energy Universe* by Gary Schwartz and her bible on Dr. Bach's flower essences approach, *Bach Flower Therapy Theory and Practice*, by Mechthild Scheffer.

All seemed to understand that nature is not only a part of who earth beings are, but is also an omnipotent part of their physical, emotional and spiritual health. There was a time when this was simply the way life was viewed, but in the drive for objective and technological knowledge, the inner relationship with the healing resources of the natural world was not only relegated to the back of the bus, it was often times not even let on.

But it was Dr. Bach's description of how flower essences raise a being's vibration and open channels to the Spirit Self that still moved her: They cure not by attacking disease, but by flooding the being with the particular virtue needed and washing out that which is causing harm. They are able, like beautiful music or any glorious uplifting thing that gives us inspiration, to raise our very natures.

Grabbing her pen and notebook, Sharon made some notes on vibrational medicine. One day she hoped to write a book about the essences she'd studied, harvested and prepared for animals: "We live in a vibratory universe. A flower essence is the energetic fingerprint of a particular flower's life force. Its healing effects are similar to those of hearing a moving piece of music: Its good vibrations fill you with positive energy. In addition to introducing a pattern of harmony into a being's system, essences also reverse dissonance and provide a missing frequency. For instance, an animal who has been abandoned and abused may never have experienced love from either their mother or their caretakers. She may become withdrawn, depressed and spirit damaged. One may gently urge such an animal toward a healthy vibration by giving her an essence formula that opens her heart to love, trust and releases past trauma."

Sharon turned her head toward the bowl holding the Castle Lake azalea, then back to her notebook. As she wrote "Castle Lake azalea treats this condition well," her thoughts drifted to Lily. Once a feral cat in the neighborhood, Lily decided to homestead Sharon's place a couple of years ago. Not long after that, she had to readjust again when Sharon moved to the foundation, where six cats already claimed residence. To help her with the transitions each time, Sharon put Castle Lake azalea flower essence in her drinking water. The healing balm soothed Lily's irritability and aloofness.

But other animals besides her own were using the flower essences. Each day brought more people, via drop-ins, phone calls and letters seeking Sharon's expanding expertise. Coupled with her animal communication skills, the therapeutic flower formulas were also being used to complement conventional animal care.

Draining the sunlight-charged liquid free of the blossoms, Sharon finished the last stages of the flower essence recipe. She put the potentized extract into a quart jar containing a stabilizer. With the mother essence now complete, many tinctures could be made.

Back in her room, Sharon unloaded the bottles, adding to the 100 single- and multiflower potions she'd already formulated. A long-time friend, Mary St. Marie, who was at the foundation for the evening meditation, watched. She asked if Sharon had ever thought of going into business, offering her services as a consultant in animal healing. "No," Sharon replied, she had not. She was just content making the essences and helping the animals. Besides, she knew nothing about running a business, and she certainly had no money to start one. Mary wouldn't let Sharon discard the business idea, reminding her that she couldn't stay at the foundation forever. She suggested Sharon ask herself one thing as she centered herself for her contemplation tonight, "How can I make a living doing something I love?"

Later, as she settled into her meditation, visions about organizing a business around the flower essences flooded her image screen. Nonstop, the graphics rendered specifics as meticulous as the color of the bottles (blue) and the size of the bottles to hold the mother essence dilution. Names of contacts, like the Flower Essence Society, were typed out before her. As the information ended, she opened her eyes. Knowing that thought precedes form, she also opened her mind and her heart to the next level of her life.

For the next few months, she explored all the facets of starting up and running a business. She might know all the roots and blossoms of flower essences, but she was a novice at the nuts and bolts of molding a

passion into a physical structure that was financially and efficiently productive. A business entrepreneur at middle age! She didn't even know
how to work a computer, much less own one. Yet, the idea felt so right
and so familiar. As if on cue, scenes from the NDE awoke in her mind.

In truth, the experience was never far away, especially when her
feline witnesses were around. And though Lily was the stalwart gate-
keeper, it was Shoji who, like a dependable insurance policy, held the
energy of the mystical encounter. Her love for her animal companions
soared beyond words; it could only be defined by the depth of her feelings. And that was fathomless.

But Sharon's reliance on her companions would be sliced in half.
Shoji, waiting for her diligently one afternoon by the heavily trafficked
street, was hit by a truck and killed. Grief stricken, Sharon's interest in
setting up an animal-healing enterprise met its own head-on collision.
Her heart, already scarred by earlier quick exits of those she loved
profoundly—her sweet daughter, her gregarious dad—now ached with
relentless sorrow, leaving no room for any other feeling.

With Shoji gone, she began to doubt all, including her once-facile
ability to communicate with her feline friend. She had not heard from
him since his physical death two days ago. Never had she so ached for
animal conversation.

But another pain threatened to smother her: guilt. Forgetting that
Shoji had his own life plan and purposes, Sharon blamed herself for her
animal companion's death. Like clothes tossing over and over in a hot
dryer, she reproached herself repeatedly: Why hadn't she paid better
attention to the whole situation? Wouldn't her beloved Shoji, who knew
no strangers and was adored by all, still be here if she had? No matter
how hard she tried to center herself and feel the bulwark energy of the
NDE's alpine meadow, she could not connect to its images and feelings.
Depression shrouded her with its heavy darkness. Crying herself into a
concave numbness the third night, she felt the room change. Within its
translucent light, a recognizable presence materialized. A handsome
gray cat, centered and serene, faced her. Shoji! Shoji told her to please
understand his death was not tragic; it was just the opposite. Knowing
he could better help Sharon on the other side, he had crossed over to
give her human friend imperative information and to elbow her closer
to the playing out of her Divine blueprint.

With sharp visual detail, he then telepathically instructed Sharon how to proceed with the flower essence business, beginning with the making of the essences. Every step was defined—what flowers to include, the kind of bowl to use for the imprint transfer, the timing and meditation process, how to store the bowls during the essence-making trips and how to bless them once she brought them home. Their formula names would reflect their purposes: Return to Joy, Recovery, Special Stress, Harmony, Fur and Feather, Service Animals, Tranquility, Expanded States, St. Francis Formula, Christ Consciousness. Under his guidance, he promised her, more formulas would follow in time.

Shoji then revealed the name of the company and the product icon. Anaflora Flower would be symbolized by St. Frances surrounded by a Siberian Husky, a gray tabby, two white doves and Mt. Shasta in the background.

Shoji also assured her, as long as she refused to buy in to the fears of her rational mind, the funds to finance Anaflora would find their way to her door. As always, she need only listen and trust. But now, although he would always be a part of her, she must let him go; it would not be fair to either of them to hang on. Animals, like humans, have their own blueprints to fulfill and must not wait for their human companions to cross over to continue the journey. Besides, they would never really be separated because love is egoless and has no boundaries. As for his job of holding Sharon's NDE memories, Lily now held that responsibility. Shoji asked only that when Sharon harvested the Siskiyou iris, she think of him. In his playful fashion, he added that he sent her purrr-fect love.

When the phone rang a few days later, she stopped for a moment when the caller identified himself as Bill's brother. It had been a long interlude since she had heard from her first husband. Never a part of their family's fabric, Bill had tried to thread his way back into their daughter's life a few times when Jennifer was a teen. But, though he was welcomed, he would flutter in and out, never staying long. After Jennifer's unsolved disappearance, he surfaced again via the occasional phone call to Sharon. For the first time, they got to know one another on a different level; they became friends. But now the talks would end: Bill was dead from cancer, leaving her his computer and $18,000.

Later that afternoon, as she set out on her daily walk around town, she mulled over the somber news. Once again death had stumbled into her life, bringing with it not only loss, but also latent blessings. Thanks to Bill's gift, Anaflora could now become a business to help animals and their caretakers. Just as Shoji had assured her, her animal communication talents and her flower essence knowledge would be the fodder for her own new beginning. If only her father could see her now. She *could* make a living just hanging around with animals.

As she rounded a corner to head down Mt. Shasta Boulevard, she felt a pull towards a secondhand clothing shop. Though she knew the proprietor (in a small town everyone knew everyone else), this was different. Stepping inside, she saw two teens gathered around a third, who had something on her finger. All were discussing how the tiny animal folded her front legs as if she was praying. "That's how she got her name," one girl said authoritatively. "But what was she doing here?" asked another. She'd read they like warmer and moister places, not like here at Mt. Shasta where it's so dry and cool.

LISA METZGER

With her flower essence creations, Sharon added the power of flowers to her intuitive work with dogs and all the planet's creatures.

Sharon walked closer and saw the praying mantis. At first, she was simply alarmed, thinking the teens would be careless with the insect. But when she spoke with them and they talked about their plans to release this "cool bug" back to nature, she felt assured for the animal's safety. But it was her direct communication with the serene little creature that comforted her the most, as a childhood memory sprang up. She could see and feel herself talking with a female praying mantis, whom she'd saved from the family cat, and who, in turn, had promised to help Sharon one day. That day was today, for with this praying mantis before her, Sharon knew the insect's presence was a sign that the direction she was headed was most assuredly up.

With a nod of recognition, the praying mantis before her said that was indeed why she was here. Sharon was to move forward with the Anaflora business and her work as an animal empath. The praying mantis also had a reminder from the animals on the other side. As she began to paint the next page in her Divine blueprint, Sharon should be ever mindful of the stories the animals tell, "for we all are colorful storytellers at heart, and in our stories you will receive the messages of Universal Truths to share with our human companions, starting with The Real Thing."

As she thanked the praying mantis with her heart, and the teenagers aloud for taking good care of him, she said her goodbyes to all. She stepped out into the late, subdued light of the day. She felt a renaissance in her soul. There was much to do. With her crayons in hand, she was ready.

6

THE STORYTELLERS

Although she didn't say much the Whale did
talk on important occasions. The first time
the Boy heard her was when he wondered
out loud if whales could jump. "Yes, we can
jump," said the Whale . . . . From that day
the Whale used to tell him stories.

The Boy and the Whale, José Maria Sanchez-Silva

*S*ince that meeting with the praying mantis, Anaflora was
becoming a reality. With the money she'd inherited from Bill,
along with the computer, meditation and the support of
friends, the pieces were fitting together like a jigsaw puzzle.
Sharon's physical health was improving, too. Though she'd been a vege-
tarian since her early 20s, she became even more particular about her
diet. The animals made it very plain that they would not talk freely with
her if she ate them. Besides keeping her meals animal free, she also eliminated processed foods, aware that a cleaner physical body sharpened
her perception to all kinds of energy.

Besides nourishing her physical body, she set out to feed her spiritual body. Although she had eschewed the dogma of Catholicism for its

view of animals, she continued to embrace part of her childhood religion: saints and angels. Both were expressions of the mystical arm of Christianity. Mystical Christianity, with its foundation in individual enlightenment and union with God without interference, spoke to her.

In her mid-20s, she had been led to Tibetan Buddhism. She resonated with its of view of life, one based on kindness and compassion toward all living things. The spiritual tradition believed in the principle of cause and effect in everyday actions; what you put out there comes back to you. Coupled with karma was also the belief in reincarnation. From there, her spiritual awareness expanded to include Taoism, Zen Buddhism and Sufism, a pure form of Islam with no religious rules. All offered stories of mystics who dedicated themselves to not only finding their own connection to the God Source, but also their life purposes.

But, as beautiful as many of these teachings were, she preferred to affix none of their labels to her spiritual identification. Believing that ideologies and creeds tended to create barriers, she adhered to no set philosophies. Her only stance was that life was a Divine gift and a Divine experience. To know its richness fully was to be aligned with one's blueprint, and to live in the moment with great compassion, gratitude, joy and service to all beings. Being still, not attending to the chatter of the world, was another critical element in her life. In meditation, she not only reconnected to her Spirit Self and her Guidance, but she also listened to the pulse of the Universe.

The NDE helped mold those principles. During that time, she felt the lightness of being egoless. There was no "I," no "good fences make good neighbors." With unconditional love as the glue, everyone and everything was a part of the whole. As she eventually settled back into her physical body, the ego-self took over the driver's seat. But she was accepting of its resurgence, knowing that the ego keeps one grounded, a necessity in maintaining a functional physical existence. Yet she was thankful to have seen beyond the veil to the real world, the one that operates on the highest vibration of all things and all beings.

When she read, she turned to words that not only informed her, but also uplifted her. Her home had no TV, radio or conventional periodicals or newspapers. Instead, books from her childhood, *Beautiful Joe, Charlotte's Web* and *The Velveteen Rabbit* were at her hand. Other oft-consulted books included those written by several of her favorite spiritual writers: Andrew Harvey, the author of *The Direct Path*, a

scholar of mystical traditions and the spiritual value of animals; Father
Bede Griffiths, who merged Christianity with Hinduism and taught
about the unity of all religions; and Joel Goldsmith, her daily fountain
of inspiration, an inspirational writer and American mystic who took
his Christian Scientist background to a higher level.

Along with reading, helping people with their animals and staying
close to a small number of friends, she maintained a solitary life. Having
made a definitive decision when she'd left David three years ago not to
seek male companionship until she was on a first-name basis with her
inner self, she had instead focused on making flower essences and growing spiritually. Not that she didn't have a few male platonic friends.
Fatah, so vivacious with his long hair and expressive face, could always
be counted on to drop by to discuss books and metaphysical ideology;
his dishes of food left on her doorstep when she was ill had kept her fed
more than once. With his encouragement, she'd even attended a couple
of small public gatherings to reacquaint herself with being around people again. When he suggested that she serve as a ticket taker at a music
concert in a friend's home, she agreed.

During a lull at the entrance door, she stepped away to survey the
hills around her, inhaling the intense smell of the fir and pine trees.
Climbing up the path to the house from a distance, a familiar figure
caught her eye. Quite pleased to have a chance to surprise Fatah, she hid
behind a pine. But when she jumped out with a silly face and a "boo,"
she was the one surprised. The man wasn't Fatah, but someone whom
she didn't know! Embarrassed, she apologized, but as he smiled and
walked away, she knew she had seen him somewhere before. And then
she remembered. With a long, flowing mane and sparkling blue eyes, he
had stood out in more than one of her childhood dreams and more
recently in the NDE. Without a doubt, she knew this man was meant
to be in her life. She'd finally met—and with quite a fanfare—her life
partner! But he obviously didn't share this prescient recognition, as he
accepted her apology, smiled and walked on into the concert.

Feeling giddy and awkward as a teenager, she hoped to talk with
him later. But that didn't happen. A few weeks later she saw him again
at another social event. But again, he left before they could talk beyond
a few words. The local coffee shop finally drew the two together. Seeing
him at a table writing in a journal, she strolled over to him. Weak-
kneed, she sat down. They talked about a poem he'd only just written,

and she found herself telling him about her NDE. A week later, he came for supper. And never left.

A former aerospace engineer with business acumen, Perusha Ananda's skill in getting Anaflora off the launching pad was the third stage in the formation of the animal communication and flower essence business. His work as a musician, spiritual seeker and teacher also absorbed his time. With a small house serving as their living and office space, Sharon and Perusha soon were working long hours. She answered the phones, set up the appointments and gave the animal communication consultations; he handled the bookkeeping and general business operations.

As word spread about Sharon's skills, her reputation as a decoder of animal behaviors and feelings picked up velocity. It was not unusual for the phones to ring at all hours with requests from people seeking answers about the animals in their lives. Professional relationships with veterinarians and other animal health care specialists also continued to flourish, and after publication of her articles on animals in several magazines, the business mushroomed even more. A part of Sharon was amazed at the flurry, yet a part was not. With each turn in her life's journey, she had been guided to offer this service for the animals and their human caretakers. Surely this is what it meant to be aligned with one's Divine blueprint.

As the days expanded into weeks and the weeks into years, a pattern emerged with the consultations. Sharon listened first to the caller's concerns about his or her animal companion, then merging with the animals, she opened her heart and mind to their individual styles of communication. Some animals spoke with visual images, some with transferred thoughts, some mixed pictures and concepts, but every one communicated in the natural language of all beings: soul talk. By connecting to the animals' core self and feeling what they were feeling, she listened to their stories.

The animals were exceptional storytellers. Though occasionally she'd meet a few animals who were reluctant to talk at the onset of a reading. One horse even directed her thoughts to a 16th-century axiom: "A man may well bring a horse to the water, but he cannot make him drink without the will." Responding with laughter, she'd assured the horse, as she did all reticent creatures, that she respected their silence and had no ego-bound desire to have them communicate if that was not their desire. That assurance usually lifted their veils and the stories flowed, for they, like all the animals with whom Sharon chatted, treasured an opportunity to talk without restraint from the heart to one who truly listened without conditions or judgment.

From their stories, she gleaned germane information about their lives and their sacred purposes for being on earth. One purpose in particular interlaced every account. The animals conveyed to her that their relationship with humankind was based on love, a spiritual tie that knows no knots and no severance. With that mystical bond comes a hallowed responsibility: it was their job to serve as authentic mirrors to their human companions and to bring messages of Universal Truths. By speaking in the language of reflection, a natural language that is projected from one being to another, the animals said that they encouraged people to grow in spirit by reflecting their emotions, thoughts and behaviors back to them. With messages of Universal Truths, they offered wise counsel in living a balanced, compassionate life, fully aware of one's Divine blueprint.

PERUSHA ANANDA

With stories from this Arctic Fox cub and other animals, Sharon understood that animals serve as mirrors to their human companions, encouraging them to grow in spirit.

Often, after communicating with an animal, the memory of the creatures' words in the alpine meadow—"We will remain deeply connected, and through our kind back on your planet, messages of Universal Truths will ring out. You need only listen."—drifted back to her. As time brought more and more animal storytellers Sharon's way, her appreciation toward them and their steadfast devotion to the Homo sapiens of this planet only widened.

She began keeping a personal journal of the storytellers, recording their messages of spiritual wisdom and love. Each reflections-of-the-heart narrative shone with radiant truth, compassion and light, starting with the journal's first three stories: a Border Collie in Alaska, a bay horse in New York State and an orange tabby in Oregon.

7

THE REAL THING

"Real isn't how you are made," said the Skin Horse. "It's a thing that happens to you when a child loves you for a long, long time, not just to play with, but REALLY loves you, then you become Real."

The Velveteen Rabbit, Margery Williams

Callie knew it wouldn't be long now before Rudy would put in his two cents' worth. Sprawled in front of the TV, her head on the dog's sinewy belly layered with rich fur, the six-year-old, watching *The Lady and the Tramp* for the umpteenth time, waited expectantly.

When the forlorn dogs held captive in the city pound appeared on the screen, the alert black and white Border Collie sat up, ready for the vocal number. As the video characters opened their mouths and launched a midnight lament, Rudy joined the howling ensemble with a majestic baritone.

Erupting in giggles, the 35-pound girl lassoed her animal companion with her arm, bringing him down in a smothering hug. Like a bingo hopper cascading over and over, the two friends rolled on the floor. Rudy welcomed the chance to play the twirling game; however, he refused to end his raucous song, which fueled Callie's efforts to hassle him even more.

Only when Callie's mother reminded the little girl that bedtime was near and she had to pick up her toys and books did the wrestling match end. In an ongoing conversation with Rudy, Callie went about her task. With his help, Callie plucked the stray items around the house, placing them in their designated places in her bedroom. With teeth brushed and pajamas on, the little girl and her animal companion snuggled together in the bay window, peering out into the night and making plans for tomorrow.

After her parents came in with their good nights, she in the top bunk bed and Rudy in the lower, they continued their talks. Though she found she didn't really have to *say* anything to communicate with him; they could talk with their hearts and minds. That's how close they were. Their telepathic conversations were as ordinary as the snow that surrounded their home.

Her mother said they'd always been that way. When Callie was born, the canine had already been a part of the family for four years. Purchased in Illinois, a long way from their home here in Alaska, Rudy was brought back to serve as a companion to her mother. Callie's dad traveled a lot and, though their farm had sled dogs, her mom wanted a dog inside with her while he was away.

Growing into a 45-pound dog, with high white socks on his legs and a big white *y* on his head, Rudy was the epitome of intelligence, dedication and agility. And once Callie joined the family, those laudable qualities seemed to leap out even more, as he became the little girl's protector and friend.

Leaning over and looking down on Rudy from the top bunk, Callie asked Rudy if he remembered the first time he saw her. Although the dog replied with two succinct yelps, the youngster relayed once again the story her parents had told her.

The day Callie was to come home from the hospital, her father had placed an infant seat securely on the back seat of the family four-by-four vehicle. But before he could shut the door to drive away, Rudy, clench-ing a colorful object in his teeth, bounded into the car. In a hurry, her dad told the collie he had to get out. He didn't want to be late. But Rudy refused. Instead he tried to jump into the back seat. Finally succeeding, the dog deposited the green ball, his favorite, into the carrier. Sealing his welcoming gift with a lick and a paw pat, he then vaulted out of the car. It was his way of welcoming her to the family.

Soon Callie was filling the room with other chronicles from their early days together, reminding the dog of such legendary times as when he saved her from a long fall down the stairs by grabbing her diaper. Or funny times when she'd refused to let her parents wash her face, but allowed Rudy's big tongue to do so.

He had let her dress him up for a big wedding and walked down the aisle with her, and he'd faithfully follow behind her horse when she was riding.

Rudy, stretched out on his side below, with ears in active sonar mode, listened attentively. Speaking softly, she told him that she knew he did all that because they were going to be what they were right now: best friends forever.

After home schooling the next day, the petite blue-eyed blonde girl and the omnipresent dog played while they waited to help Callie's mom with chores. For the two, playing was just another form of communicating. There was treasure hunting, dramatized by digging and falling in the surrounding snow banks; chase, today played with balloons ready for the popping; Frisbee, a game that could, if Rudy missed a toss, end up being a treasure-hunt game again; classic hide-and-seek; and long walks around the family's 20-acre home place.

Yet, Rudy knew how to work as hard as he knew how to play with ebullience. Around the farm, as well as the animal rehabilitation center Callie's mother ran, the dog would assist by herding, fetching and training. Though there was a slight hitch to the former.

A natural herder, the Border Collie could be relied on to usher wayward animals to their places from the pasture or from area to area inside the center. Except sheep. Instead of gathering them and directing them to the barn, Rudy persisted in vaulting over their wooly bodies. Each time the family would give him another chance to connect to his genetic calling, the Border Collie would quickly detour from any herding attempts and, with great gusto, return to sailing over the sheep.

The scene never failed to make Callie laugh. Trying to muffle her amusement, Callie would run to her pal to remind him he need only herd the sheep as he did the cows and horses. After all, she'd tell him, he wasn't competing in an agility-and-hurdles contest. He should save that for when he competed around the state in agility competitions.

A regional winner, Rudy, like a canine Jesse Owens, was a supple hurdler. His adroitness was known as far south as Anchorage, and after coming out on top at yet another meet, Rudy would rush to collect his hugs from Callie. Her glee would often extend to telling anyone near her favorite story about the "failed" but winning sheep dog. During one race, the collie, apparently forgetting—or perhaps giving himself an extra challenge—that he'd already sailed over one hurdle, returned to the far obstacle and shot over it again. He still outran all his opponents with ease and captured another blue ribbon.

At home, fetching and sorting was another easy task for the intelligent dog. From being told to go for something and dispersing it where instructed, to managing his own balls and plastic squeaky frogs, Rudy was the dependable helper. He was just as proficient at staying clear of activities that his presence could hinder, such as clearing the land or feeding the horses.

But it was Rudy's training skills that Callie's mother consistently counted on. Always the role model for the other dogs, Rudy, though not a husky, was adept at training the puppies to mush. Leading the young dogs, the collie, following vocal commands, as well as the pull of the reins, was the alpha dog; however, once the new crew had the routine down pat, Rudy would sit shotgun by Callie's mother. In the front seat of the sled, the two would traverse the landscape listening to the tape deck. Sometimes on their trips, Callie's mother would take her skis and ski away from the sled. When she whistled, Rudy would head out to her with the team in tow.

But Rudy was happiest when he was with Callie. In her room at night, Callie would often pull one of her favorite books from the bookshelf and read aloud the story. Even her walls, in a colorful calligraphy mural, depicted the tale of *The Velveteen Rabbit*.

Callie loved the book because it explained best how she felt about Rudy. She considered the faithful dog the most real being around her. She could tell him, whether verbally or telepathically, her secrets, her fears and her delights. With unfathomable and unconditional acceptance, he loved beyond the barriers of her everyday life. She could not picture life without him, for in the sometimes confusing adult world, he was her only true friend.

But she didn't have to worry. He'd promised her he'd never leave her. And he was a dog of promises. Whether given or kept ones, he was always teaching her the importance of promises. When she couldn't play ball with him, all she had to do was tell him when they could. He'd remember and keep the date. Yesterday, she told him they'd play ball at noon. At 12:00, he came to her with the green ball, ready to play fetch. As always, he kept his promise, and she kept hers.

But as Callie closed her eyes to sleep this snowy evening, Rudy communicated to her that the biggest one was yet to come. The little girl, dropping into dreamland, did not respond.

One summer day (her dad had heard it would be a hot 73 degrees), Rudy unleashed another promise. After zooming down the slide together in the backyard, Callie and the Border Collie set out for the creek. A favorite spot, Rudy would first splash headlong into the cold water. Trying to coax Callie to join him, he'd go back and forth to her on the bank as she focused on building a dam. His splashing and her engineering duties soon resulted in two soaked play partners. Lying in the sun with Rudy, Callie draped her arm across her canine partner. As she stroked his damp fur, it occurred to her that she must be getting big, for Rudy seemed to be smaller than before. Happy that she *really* was becoming a big girl, her mind conjured up some new games they could play. Sensitive to her thoughts, Rudy jumped up and, tugging on Callie's jacket sleeve, urged her back to the house. There, he retrieved his balls, and soon a game of fetch was in motion.

Tossing the black sphere as far as her diminutive arm could project, Callie watched as Rudy the athlete went for the rubber ball. As he lunged for it, Rudy staggered, then quickly recovered, and brought the ball to Callie. But on the next throw, he lost his balance again. This time the collapse was beyond recovery. Unable to lift her friend, Callie ran for her mother.

At the veterinarian's office, the animal doctor discovered that the Border Collie had swollen lymph nodes the size of golf balls. Diagnosing Rudy with cancer, the vet suggested that the dog be put down. Refusing,

Callie's mom put Rudy back into the car. On the way home, with tears sliding down her cheeks, Callie's mother told her daughter she was sorry and not to be afraid of what could happen. With her arm around Rudy, who was sandwiched between the two females, Callie responded that she wasn't afraid; Rudy had promised her he'd always be with her.

Not sure how to answer, Callie's mom, chewing on her lip, was quiet for several minutes. Though she had noticed Rudy had seemed thinner than usual, and less spontaneous, she had dismissed any irregularity with his health as a consequence of the changing seasons. Animals often reacted to the transition in many ways. Never had she considered that Rudy was ill. Around Callie, he had seemed as robust and as attentive as ever.

As the car gobbled up the last few miles of their journey home, she announced to her little girl and her dog that she had an idea: she was going to try to get in touch with someone she'd used before with the animals in her care at her rehabilitation center. Callie asked if it were Sharon. Callie's mom nodded yes. With determination fortifying every word, Callie turned to face her mother and stated that she, too, wanted to talk with the animal communicator.

Answering the emergency request, Sharon listened as Callie's mom explained why she had called about Rudy and asked what Rudy could tell them about his situation. Merging with the Border Collie, the animal intuitive immediately connected with the dog. A visual communicator, he spoke with direct thought that employed words, as well as pictures so stunning so multihued that Sharon felt she was a child again watching for the first time a Technicolor picture show at the movie theater.

Rudy's expressions were also very humanlike in form and feeling. The dog began by communicating that though his head felt heavy and he was having trouble with balance, he was in no pain and had no medical requests. Grateful to Callie's mother that she didn't put him down at the clinic, he said that when it was time for him to go, he wanted to be at home with his family, especially Callie. He only asked that the family listen to Callie. She would know what to do.

Aware that Callie wanted to talk now, Rudy also sent a thought request to Sharon that he wished to speak to his friend. Handing the phone to her daughter, Callie's mother told her that Rudy wanted to speak with her by way of Sharon.

Holding the receiver that dwarfed her delicate face, Callie spoke with confidence. She asked Sharon if she thought animals had souls. When the animal intuitive replied that she did, the little girl said she knew they did because they were gentle, kind and good listeners. And good talkers. Though they talked in a different language than out-loud words, they talked with their hearts. "Maybe that's why," she told Sharon, "people don't listen real hard to them."

Laughing, Sharon said it was too bad Callie lived so far away; with her wisdom, she could come work with her. Interjecting, Rudy conveyed that Callie was right. The two of them did have a special bond. That was why he wanted her to listen to her heart in the coming days. He also wanted her to remember what he'd always promised her, for he loved her very much.

Over the next six weeks, as Rudy's lymph nodes under his chin ballooned and his body contracted in size, Rudy's health rapidly deteriorated. Yet, he refused to change his patterns. Though weaker and often unsteady, he stuck to his routines. When a horse got out, he headed out across the field to herd him back, and when Callie was outside, he'd urge her to play a bit or take walks.

During one of those abbreviated walks down the hill from the house, the dog and the little girl spoke their own language. Via that telepathic connection, Rudy said that if he did get too tired to go on, he wanted to be buried here, where he could see everything: the house, the windows to her room, the horses, the animal center. But mostly, he expressed to her that he wanted her to remember that if he left, he promised he'd come back. He yearned to be a Border Collie again. Stopping, she faced her pal, and with the purity of a child's trust, Callie told him then he would and she'd be looking for him.

That night, as the Border Collie rose to go to the back door to be let out to urinate, he headed straight to the hallway wall. Bumping into it, he fell back, only to get up and repeat the action. Rushing to him, Callie saw that he seemed out of focus with his surroundings.

Callie called for her mother. In a gentle, matter-of-fact manner, Callie told her that Rudy was getting ready to leave his body. Marveling, and yet wanting to disagree with her daughter's assessment, Callie's mom stood silent as she watched the pair step outside into the silvery moonlight. Watching the two near the dark blue barn, Callie's mom noticed that Rudy seemed to have taken on a translucent pearl essence. As they returned to the house, Riley, the housecat, and Paws, the outside cat, joined the duo.

Back in the house, Callie and the two felines sat by Rudy. Stroking her pal and speaking lovingly to him, Callie felt a warm, light presence in the room with them. She knew Rudy was aware of the energy too, and, in the soprano whisper of a child, asked if he could see them.

As the dog lifted his head, Callie's mother lifted the phone receiver. Hoping to reach Sharon, she dialed the emergency number. As she relayed the situation to Sharon, the animal intuitive confirmed that indeed the animal spirits were there to help Rudy during his transition. Sending blessings, Sharon said Callie and Rudy could handle it from here.

Helping her parents dig the grave the following morning, Callie had no tears. When her mother asked if she were sad, the willowy child, placing flowers on the dog's body, replied that she wasn't sad because Rudy wasn't here; he was in heaven already.

That afternoon at the state fair exhibition, as Callie and her horse, whom Rudy had helped Callie coach, warmed up, she told other riders about Rudy's passing and burial. Each time she'd end the news by stating assuredly that the Border Collie would be back. He'd promised her.

As Callie cuddled in her bed on the fourth night after her buddy's death, she looked toward the window where they had often sat together to gaze at the world outside her room. As she comforted herself with the memory, a bright light charged the room with a glow as white as the snow outside. Within its illumination, a familiar presence dominated the room. Emerging in the distinct shape of a Border Collie, Rudy appeared. His eyes full of love, he assured her he hadn't forgotten his promise. With that pledge, he disappeared into the misty light.

Quickly leaning over the edge of her bunk bed, she automatically looked down below for Rudy in his customary spot. But he was not there. Though she knew Rudy would not let her down, that he would come to her again one day to live, she wanted to be with him now. To bury her face into his Rudy-smell fur, wrap her arm around his neck and playfully wrestle him to the floor would be grand. But, most of all, she'd just like to hug him close to her. Missing him with a hollowness she had never known, Callie cried, as she would many times in the next several days.

Three years later, Callie had settled into a routine that left little time for nostalgia. Active with school, her horse and competitions, as well as the animals around the rehabilitation center, she was a busy nine-year-old. Yet, she still made it a frequent practice to visit Rudy's grave.

Sitting there on the tall grass in the summer or on the snow mound in the winter, she could still feel his energy. But one Saturday in April, she found she could not. No matter what memory she'd conjure up of Rudy, or how she'd try to communicate with her old pal, Callie felt as if the once-special place seemed almost empty and held only a shadow of Rudy's characteristic energy. But as she tried to untangle this puzzling change, Callie was interrupted by her mother's voice calling her home.

At the house, Callie's mother told her daughter she had a surprise for her inside. Opening the door to the kitchen, Callie's feet were targeted by a blur of canine black and white fur. Stumbling, the little girl landed on the tile floor. As if on cue, the bubbly greeter, a seven-week-old Border Collie puppy, pounced on Callie. The two were soon rolling on the floor in a familiar, freewheeling wrestling match.

Naming the dog Rueben, Callie began to notice things about her new animal companion. Mostly that he didn't seem new at all. He had no need to be shown the layout of the house or the family routine. From day one, he went without direction to the food dish, Callie's bedroom, the barn, the animal center and even the paths to the creek. He was equally familiar with helping Callie's mother. She could ask him to bring her something and, though never having been instructed, he'd locate the tool and take it to her.

To Callie, who never had to teach Rueben ball games or Frisbee, there was only one reason for the new dog's behavior: He was Rudy.

One act sealed Callie's belief that Rueben, except for his name and markings on his coat, was really her old friend Rudy. Deciding to play a video from her early childhood, the young girl put in *The Lady and the Tramp*. Though Rueben had never seen this movie, when the scene with the singing dogs in the pound came on, Rueben sang along exactly at the same place that Rudy had unfailingly chimed in.

Telling her mother that she knew Rudy, as he had promised, had come back, Callie said she was glad that he'd come back as a Border

Collie, just as he'd said he had wanted to do. Callie's parents, having seen Rueben's seemingly prescient knowledge about the family routine, his familiar ease with the other animals and his obvious connection to Callie, were at a loss to dispute their daughter's claims. Yet, blatantly acknowledging that Rudy was now Rueben was a big step.

On the phone with Sharon Callahan, Callie's mother asked about Rueben and Callie. Though the animal intuitive said it was a rare event for an animal to return to the same species or human family, all things were possible when it came to love. And with children and animals, and the impenetrable relationship they can have with one another, nothing was out of bounds. For the comfort that an animal companion can give a child is without limitations, and the promises they share are very real. Not just for the human, but for the animal as well.

Connecting with the animal communicator via thought transfers, Rueben conveyed to Sharon that, with his connection to Callie rooted in truth and trust, he had returned to be with Callie because he had promised. He had promised because he loved her. And genuine love, the glue of life, makes all things real.

Rudy, the Border Collie who believed in keeping promises.

That evening as Sharon completed the last reading of the day, her thoughts skipped back to the earlier session with Rueben. Mindful that animals often mirror their human companions, she considered what he, as well as Rudy, had reflected about their young friend in Alaska. Bright as Polaris in the evening sky, the answer was indisputable: The dogs' reflections were quite simply the untarnished love of a child.

That message resurfaced an endearing passage from a prized book she had kept on her shelf when she was a little girl. In *The Velveteen Rabbit*, a cloth rabbit, who yearns to be real, is told by the Skin Horse what it means to be real. "Real isn't how you are made," said the Skin Horse. "It's a thing that happens to you when a child loves you for a long, long time, not just to play with, but REALLY loves you, then you become Real."

8

THE BOND

*I only know that sometimes something does
happen between people and animals. There
seems to be a bond that overcomes all fear,
prejudice, everything objectionable.*

Gentle Ben, Walt Morey

s **the veterinarian** approached the restless, reddish-brown horse, he recalled the last time he'd tried to examine Wex. With his ears back signaling a don't-touch-me warning and his eyes flashing anger, the 17-3 hands sport horse had refused to let the animal doctor near him. Nor would the bay, recently off the boat from Ireland, let anyone easily ride him. Favoring his right rear end, Wex, acting like a fire-breathing dragon, let it be known that if anyone tried to get near, he was not going to stand for it. Right away, Dr. Alan Schoen surmised that if a horse were this reactive, he either had to be in severe pain, say a fracture, or he had been so abused that he didn't trust any human's motives. Either way, Schoen never got close enough that day to find out.

Known as an experienced blue-ribbon rider in the New England area, Rachel Granshaw was asked to work with the troubled horse. Using her equestrian skills (she rode a horse before she could walk), she was soon secure on Wex's back, and a bond began to develop between the Irish steed and the 40-year-old businesswoman, who adamantly believed that riding was all about the connection between horse and rider. But Wex didn't extend his respect to other riders who tried to mount him, and, in time, the owners, looking for a good home for the rambunctious horse, gave him to Rachel.

Yet, though he'd become more at ease with Rachel, Wex still exhibited some of his old behaviors at her stables. He was skittish when there was any activity around his stall, especially around feeding time, and he was still touchy about his rear quarter. Affection, whether receiving or giving it, was an enigma to him. And there was something else that Rachel felt about Wex, but couldn't quite rein in; she knew she had to try, starting with the physical. Pleading with Schoen to have a second go with him, she convinced the veterinarian to make another home visit.

With the horse before him, Schoen could tell he was less aggressive than the first time, but that he still had zero tolerance for anyone sidling up to his right hindquarter. With Rachel's help, he sedated Wex and examined him. Using acupuncture, he helped relieve some muscle spasms that were common to a horse being pushed when he wasn't willing to go. Aware of Rachel's firm but compassionate horsemanship, he determined the abuse had to have stemmed from Wex's youth. Other than the muscle contractions, however, Schoen could find no apparent abnormalities that might provoke Wex's troubling behavior.

After arranging for a definitive bone scan, Schoen suggested to Rachel that Wex's emotional body be addressed. He recommended that she call Sharon Callahan, an animal intuitive on the West Coast who had helped many of his clients.

With the bone scan report ruling out any physical concerns, Rachel was prepared to talk to Sharon, almost. She was smart enough to know that the rapport one had with a horse was affected by what each brought to the saddle, that is, where each stood mentally, emotionally and spiritually in their respective lives. With Wex, it was obvious where he was. He was wounded. And just where was she?

At the age of 18, her father, her hero, the one she trusted and loved more than life itself and the one she worked hard to please, had died. Rachel's relationship with her mother and her sister had already been tense from miscommunication and jealousy. A natural and award-winning rider, Rachel was her dad's favorite. Now, the relationship became taught as a new harness. For a while, she was even denied access to the family's stables. By her mid-20s, she was a professional in the corporate world, among people who were oblivious to her equestrian background. She rode sporadically, usually only when requested by former associates from the horse world, as in the case of Wex.

But being estranged the last two decades from her family and the farm, where the familiar smells of hay and manure could take her back to the warmth of her father's presence, had been creating its own fecund mash of emotions. Although she eventually was allowed to keep her horse there, her expertise in training or running the riding school was not welcomed. Hurt, disappointment, anger, uncertainty and a lack of self-confidence rode her unceasingly.

When she heard Sharon Callahan's voice, she began to feel hopeful, both for Wex and herself. She knew that this consultation would most likely have to be about more than just Wex; it would have to be about her, too. With the reassurance of Sharon's gentle voice, Rachel candidly shared her life, complete with all the emotional wrappings.

As Sharon listened to Rachel about Wex's behavioral and emotional problems, she was struck by the woman's openness, as well as her awareness that the animal in her life was a mirror to her own soul. Many times people had called to say that this horse is behaving this or that way, and if he doesn't stop, he's out the door to the glue factory. With an animal's intuitive ability to read our feelings and thoughts, this was not a positive first step to healing. Sharon would sadly end the session before it began. She simply could not work with someone who viewed an animal companion as a disposable commodity. Just as the saying "a mind is a terrible thing to waste" was of truth, so was trying to work with a mind that is drenched in negative energy. That frame of mind is not only self-destructive for the person, but it also provokes fear in the animal.

But Rachel's sincere desire to help Wex and the horse's willingness to talk opened the barn door to direct communication. As Sharon merged with Wex, she felt his readiness to be intimate with details of past abuse that took him to the emotional stresses he harbored today. Images flashed on her mind's screen of a spirit-damaged being: a painful and troubled birth, with no one there to help; harsh training to be a fox-hunting horse, with food being denied as punishment. His life as a stallion, constrained, pushed and electrically prodded to impregnate mares for human female hormones. No longer trusting humans, he began to withdraw, responding with anger and resistance. Yet, Wex, with flickers of his own divine blueprint still within him, had kept hope and a strong will afloat. Though he was anxious when he flew across the Atlantic to the Americans who'd bought him, he knew he was moving closer to meet the woman who could help him. Now that Rachel was finally his companion, he communicated to Sharon that he wanted to heal and live in the moment, with no bridles from the painful past to hold them back. For his behaviors were not just of his experiences, but, in spiritual synchronicity, true reflections of Rachel's as well.

To assist Wex in relinquishing his past and opening his heart to love, trust and bonding, Sharon suggested several Wex-communicated activities that would help him and Rachel. The animal intuitive also suggested that both consider taking flower essences for past abuse and trauma. The California Wild Rose and Bleeding Heart were especially appropriate for helping to heal negative emotions and a damaged spirit.

In the weeks following the session with Sharon, Rachel and Wex's time together took a different route. In the saddle, she began to ask him to do things he'd recoiled from in the past, including requesting him to move forward and straighten himself out as he picked up speed when she squeezed her leg against him. Out of the saddle, after she gave him his flower essence-laced peppermint, Rachel would pull up a stool near Wex's stall and read a book. Her undemanding, yet unwavering presence helped develop another layer of trust.

Each day brought improvement in his behaviors, as trust slowly began to gain territory in his heart. The once-snarling, don't-come-near-me Wex was now a calmer and more dependable horse. Within a few months, he'd been moved from the quiet back barn to the main barn where riders peppered the grounds and little girls dropped by to gaze longingly at the big bay.

Rachel was also moving forward with her own growth. Like her animal companion, she was learning to trust not only others, but, more importantly, herself. She had always shied away from expressing her true feelings, like deep anger and hurt. When she'd stumble, Wex was there to reflect that. More than once, riding partners and stable grooms had remarked that if Wex were acting testy or mad, then Rachel must be, too, as he was such a reliable mirror of her.

One day, during a dawn ride, he reflected a more decisive and less-troubled Rachel. Now able to look at life with less rancor and frustration, thanks to the transmutation she'd seen in Wex and herself, Rachel announced that she'd come to a sad but definitive resolution. She had to let go of her dreams of ever again being an integral part of the family horse business. That door would never be opened to her. But she would not ride off into the sunset without him. He could trust that, just as she knew she could trust herself to find a place for them that honored their equestrian skills and sacred companionship.

Six months later, as Dr. Schoen walked with Rachel to the barn to see Wex, he noticed that Rachel had a light skip in her walk he'd never seen before. She seemed less uptight and more in touch with herself. But it was the big horse's behavior that took his breath away, and in quite a different way. Standing next to Rachel, Wex calmly allowed the vet to exam him. Schoen found no physical maladies and, even more markedly, a 90 percent improvement in the horse's behavior. Though he was still protective of his space during feeding time, no longer were the fear-based behaviors of aggression and anger ruling the handsome animal.

As the doctor and Rachel returned to his truck, they talked more about Wex, the flower essences and the animal intuitive who made them. Not only was the bay back in the saddle with his emotions of self-love and trust, so was Rachel. She was dealing with her family. She was starting down a heart-led career path that she knew was her calling, and she was teamed up with a horse who exhilarated her. Rachel thanked the veterinarian for referring her to the animal empath.

Schoen thanked her for taking care of Wex, and agreed that Sharon Callahan definitely had a gift. Her ease in communicating with animals had proven valuable to many. More than once, when he'd eliminated physical causations, Sharon had assisted him and the clients he referred. Her commitment and attunement to all beings never ceased to humble him.

In Mt. Shasta, Sharon updated her file on Wex. The bay was mending. His relationship with Rachel, as his actions now reflected, was cementing into solid trust. Rachel's attitude and actions were also cantering onto a positive track.

Like so many of the animals who told her their stories, Wex and his devoted service to the human companion in his life was a story of real commitment. This message of unwavering loyalty that animals regularly offered sent Sharon's thoughts back to *Gentle Ben*, a childhood book about a boy and a bear he befriended: "I only know that sometimes something does happen between people and animals. There seems to be a bond that overcomes all fear, prejudice, everything objectionable."

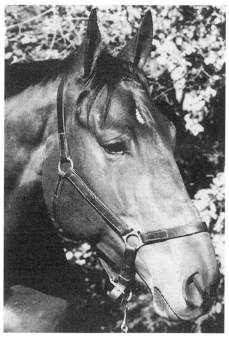

Wex, the bay stallion.

9

A PASSION FOR LIVING

Sounder ain't got no spirit left for living. . . .
He doesn't even whine anymore. He just lies
on his coffee sacks under the cabin steps.

Sounder, William H. Armstrong

If feasible, before most consultations, Sharon asked for a photo of the animal companion. A picture, indeed worth a thousand words, could often capture the signature essence of a being. In the case of Jerry the cat, it served double duty.

Holding up the picture of a girl carrying a worn Easter basket filled with a resigned, but contented, orange feline, she waited for Anne, a new client, to call. Jerry, according to the photo's notes, was the family's nine-year-old tabby and would be the subject of today's animal communication session. There was no information on the young girl, yet the animal intuitive could feel a strong bond between the youngster and the cat.

On the phone with Anne 30 minutes later, Sharon asked the woman from Oregon who the young girl holding Jerry in the photo was. Anne replied that it was her daughter Ree, at age 11. Now, Ree was 17 and in a year, she'd be out of the house, attending college in another state. Anne and her husband Richard were going to miss their only child. So would Jerry; he and Ree had been together since he was a kitten. Anne said he could tell Sharon a zillion stories about their antics and mutual affection. In fact, Jerry was the only cat Anne and Richard had ever known who'd let himself be dressed in Ree-designed clothes— and hats—and yet who'd turn around and go outside to defend his territory, always successfully, against any interlopers, including dogs.

Anne asked why Sharon wanted to know about Ree. Replying that she would broach that subject during the communication session between her and Jerry, the animal intuitive requested that Anne first express her current concerns about the feline.

Once affectionately dubbed Fat Boy, Jerry, Anne explained, was now thin, lethargic and disinterested in his old pursuits. He was also persistently licking a spot on his leg, leaving the area bald. She'd taken him to the veterinarian, but blood and urine tests, as well as a detailed exam, revealed that the cat had no physical problems.

Yet, Anne continued, Dr. Donna didn't dismiss her patient's disease. She said that experience had shown her that there was more to an animal than the physical; there was the emotional, the mental and the spiritual. Pointing out that Jerry was acting as if he were both stressed and depressed, she suggested Anne try to find out what was going on inwardly with her animal companion. The vet told her about Sharon.

Assuring Anne that she would connect with Jerry if he were willing, Sharon now centered herself for the reading. Within moments, she merged with the feline. Communicating with feelings and direct thoughts, Jerry welcomed Sharon to his mind and heart, as the animal companion showed her pictures of life inside the family dynamic.

Before transferring any of this information to Anne, however, the animal communicator shared a central characteristic about the feline species: although all animals have superb sonar when it comes to picking up the thoughts, as well as the physical and emotional feelings, of their human companions, cats are particularly vibrationally sensitive. She pointed out that they will do everything possible to nudge their human friends toward keeping their lives in balance, including mirroring their behaviors, emotions and beliefs. They, like all animal companions, take this responsibility to heart.

Jerry was no different. In fact, Sharon pointed out, as a member of the Order of the Orange—a society of orange tabbies whose focus is working with the spiritual—Jerry's connection to his human partners was intense. Always in tune with his human family, the thoughts and images he now projected to Sharon were full of details, beginning with his relationship with Ree. They grew up together; they played together. An enthusiastic human companion with a joyful and generous spirit, Ree was easy to be with. From playing chase to playing "school" (he was indeed an attentive pupil) to being Ree's fashion model, sporting the latest outfit she'd sewn by hand for him (though she didn't insist he wear them outside the house; she seemed to understand it wouldn't fit his top-cat image), they were buddies. Even when he'd do some things that bothered Ree a bit, such as delivering lizards, mice and the occasional large palmetto bug to the doorstep, she would not fuss at him.

When she became a teenager, they stayed close. Bringing friends home from school, she never failed to introduce him. But soon that would all change, as his dearly loved human companion would soon be headed for college.

Not only would he miss Ree (and she him, though in a more subtle way since she was the one leaving for a new adventure, not the one left behind), but Anne and Richard would also feel the ache in their hearts in a big way. In fact, they already were, but not openly. And, as their mirror, it was his job to show them their unacknowledged grief. With his low spirits and his current disinterest in his regular routine—even eating often didn't seem worth the effort—he was mirroring their subdued feelings of sorrow.

As the animal intuitive relayed the feline's message to her, Anne acknowledged that perhaps Jerry was indeed mirroring an unspoken sadness in the house. They had always been, even during Ree's teenage years, a tight trio. And though she and Richard had always encouraged Ree to be independent and rely on her own abilities, the change in the human family dynamic from three to two was going to take some getting used to. Jerry was right: being an empty nester was going to sting more than she'd ever conceded, and she needed to look at her own sadness.

Transferring scenes to Sharon of his lying close to a woman in a bed, Jerry continued his communication. The feline said it was not the only reason for his current physical and emotional condition. He was also tired from a three-year vigil with Anne. Underlining again that it was his job, and that he wouldn't have it otherwise, the orange tabby explained that his dedication to Anne during her recent struggle with her health had taken its toll. And while he had never doubted she'd one day heal, maintaining that energetic field of intended health with her— as all caregivers know—had been stressful and draining.

Interrupting the reading once more, Anne confirmed to Sharon that Jerry had indeed been with her through three years of a debilitating illness. Once a hard-driven documentary producer who worked incessantly, she had been sliced into humble pie with chronic fatigue syndrome. Enervated, unable to work or even think without fog taking over, Anne was forced to spend much of her time in a place she was not familiar with before the syndrome struck: bed. It was there that she and Jerry had bonded. Except when he was eating, using his litter box or visiting with Ree, the dutiful cat had affixed himself to Anne's side without intermission.

No matter when she'd wake, she'd be greeted by the gentle, yellow-eyed gaze of the warm, purring tabby. He seemed to not only feel her pain, but also his presence and his healing energy seemed to will her to get better and assure her that all was going to be okay, that one day she'd be able to feel productive and strong again. Jerry's undying devotion was noted by everyone in the family. Even Tootsie Rollie, Jerry's Siamese feline buddy, whom he adored, would have to join him on the bed if she wanted some licks from Anne's faithful sitter.

Pointing out that although her husband and Ree were extremely supportive during this time, Anne told Sharon that she couldn't emphasize enough the contribution Jerry had made to getting her well. There was always something incredibly encouraging and mystical about Jerry's stoical company.

With him, she felt no guilt, even though her Protestant work ethic was pounding at her head as much as the physical aches were pounding her body. Nor did she feel any need to explain or defend the mysterious ailment that not only required copious hours of sleep from her, but that also short wired her mind, leaving her unable to focus on things for more than a few minutes. Reading and crossword puzzles, once her bed-time joys, were no longer an option. All through the illness, Jerry stayed right there, demanding nothing from her.

With his support, Anne told Sharon, she also learned to connect again to her physical body and to let go of the anger she had toward the illness. But the best gift Jerry gave her was helping her reconnect with her core, her Spirit Self.

Serving as a role model, the feline showed her how to be content with just being still and tuning into the Zone, that special place of Light and Love that unites all in the Universe. Before, she'd thought cats spent a good deal of their day napping, but Jerry taught her that looks could be deceiving. Instead of snoozing, cats were often linking up with the Universe. Evidently, Anne laughed, his species was practicing Zen long before the Chinese and Japanese!

Besides hooking up with the Universe through meditation and prayer, Anne confessed, she also began keeping a dream journal, as well as a thoughts journal, to understand more about herself and her own journey. As she began to heal, her writing became less cryptic and more detailed; by the end of the illness, she'd filled seven books.

Each time she wrote, Jerry was there encouraging her, even when she'd just think about writing, but wouldn't pick up the pen. Butting her with his head, Jerry would pester her until she grabbed the blank book from the bedside table and started scribbling.

And now that she was well, and writing for a living again, Anne said she knew much of the credit for her return to the land of the living went to her animal companion. Asking Sharon to thank Jerry for his dedication and support, Anne waited for Jerry to continue his commu-nication with the animal intuitive.

But the feline said he had no more to add, except to tell Anne that what he did he did with love and a duty to honor his life purpose: being there for her.

As Sharon delivered Jerry's parting words, she told Anne that Jerry's commitment to his life purpose not only consumed much of his strength, but also added to the depletion of his body and life force. In other words, Sharon explained, her animal friend's spirit for living was ebbing. Depression had set in. For animals, just like humans, suffer from the full range of emotions, depression included.

Replying that she knew he'd always been a serious and tenacious cat, Anne said she'd never realized how tenacious his allegiance to the family was. Though, with her own work principles so entrenched, she probably shouldn't be surprised.

Suggesting that Anne take a look at all Jerry had generously and lovingly shown her, Sharon proposed positive emotions and deeds Anne might incorporate into her life from the mental video the feline had communicated to her. Sharon also suggested flower essence therapy. Shasta Star Tulip centered on emotions rising from family changes; Columbine, on self-appreciation. Nature's native balms, both could be helpful for everyone in the household, not just Jerry, the family mirror. Already familiar with flower essences, Anne readily agreed.

Within three months, Anne left an email with the Anaflora Web site saying that Jerry was spry again. But a year later, Anne set up another appointment with Sharon. Once again, her beloved orange cat was losing weight, was acting depressed and dispirited and was uncharacteristically clingy.

As the consultation got underway, Sharon asked if there were any changes in the household. Not really. Ree was doing fine in college, staying in close touch with the family; Richard's business was going well; she and he were still happy as a couple after 25 years of marriage. Though, she had to admit, it was hard on everyone when Tootsie Rollie, Jerry's Siamese buddy, had passed. But that had been several months ago.

As Sharon merged with Jerry, she felt his sadness over Tootsie Rollie's death. He projected picture thoughts of a sweet and loving Siamese dozing beside him. But he communicated that his biggest disappointment centered around his inability to help Anne get in sync with her spiritual blueprint, especially when it came to using her creative talents.

Though she was writing again, she was not creating works that came from her heart, works that she had come to earth to do. Since it was his sacred job to ensure she journey in that direction, he blamed himself and felt discouraged and depressed. Aware that his time on earth was not infinite—unusual, Sharon told Anne, as most animals live in the present—he also felt the squeeze of linear time. His dedication to Anne was strong. He wanted to complete his sacred purpose and not let her down.

Sharon's communiqué from Jerry didn't surprise Anne. Always in her lap when she was writing on her computer, the tabby was her muse. He seemed to edit her work with his body posture: a relaxed feline body usually corresponded with a natural, from-the-heart writing flow. As for her Divine purpose, Anne admitted that, although she was adamant about her daily meditations and keeping her dream journals, there were times she wondered about the relevance of her work. And in all honesty, she lately had become down about her purpose in life, wondering not only if she really had one, but also if she were indeed fulfilling it.

Writing, she knew, was her calling, but she also knew she wasn't writing about things that spoke to her heart. Yet, she felt the need to accept other writing demands that came her way for financial reasons. That inner conflict often dragged her down. Guess her Fat Boy was mirroring her own quiet anguish and self-disappointment.

Gently urging Anne to stay on course with her desire to connect with her life's purpose, Sharon reminded her that this would bolster Jerry's sense of well-being. Years of experience had shown her, the animal intuitive explained, that when one addressed head-on without blinking, his own issues, his animal companion's health or behavior often cleared up. That was the beauty of the symbiotic human-animal relationship.

Three months later, Anne called back to report that Jerry was gaining weight and his spirits were up. Working on an article now about finding one's purpose in life, she said she and Jerry were glued once again to the computer keys. She did the word processing; Jerry, as lap advisor, provided the encouragement.

Jerry, Order of the Orange.

As Sharon entered the orange tabby's story into her journal, she pondered the message Jerry had reflected with his emotional behaviors. Animals, like people, feel the pull of a heavy heart, and can suffer depression as they mirror their human friends' despair.

Jerry's story reminded Sharon of another animal companion who mirrored his human family's deep melancholy. From the moving children's book *Sounder,* she recalled the passage about the sorrowful dog: "Sounder ain't got no spirit left for living. . . . He doesn't even whine anymore. He just lies on his coffee sacks under the cabin steps."

10

PURE MOTIVES

Accompanying each one of those lessons was the
indirect but important reminder that he and
almost all other animals, except those spoiled
by human association, always live out from a
pure heart, that is from, pure motives.

Kinship with All Life, J. Alan Boone

s a solitary kid growing up in the Adirondacks, Paul blanketed his mind in the cold winter and fanned his thoughts in the humid summer with the writings of Plato and the stories of mythology.

And now six decades later, so much of that early interest in forms and legends was returning to him in the shape of one of the five perfect platonic forms: the dodecahedron. With its 12 sides, each in the shape of a pentagon, the structure, he believed, could be the solution to solving his animal companions' residential riddle, which he'd been working on for several months now.

Since 1973, when he obtained his first hives, he'd been getting to know the European honeybee, Apis mellifera. Tending to them with uncompromising care, he soon developed a sweet affinity for the membrane-winged creatures. It was an avocation that kept the backyard beekeeper fascinated.

Amazed at the bees' tireless efforts to sustain their hive—two million flower visits produced just one pound of honey—Paul became familiar not only with their well-perfected system of socialization and communication but also with their family dynamics: the reproductive queen bee, the hundreds of fertile male drones and the thousands of infertile female workers.

But there was something else that also expanded the apiarist's appreciation for the industrious creatures. With the ancient records of Greece, Rome, Egypt and China, as well as the Talmud, Bible, Hindu and Celtic writings, citing bees and their medicinal honey, he came to understand why many cultures considered bees Divine messengers. Dedicated to the highest good for all, their altruistic actions benefited not only their own kind, but also the planet. As one of nature's steadfast pollinators, the humble, often forgotten, honeybee was undeniably crucial to the earth's survival.

And the numbers proved it. Through further research, Paul learned that commercial honeybees, trucked farm to farm, pollinate 90 crops in the United States alone, one-third of the food consumed annually. Transporting the hives to the fields was necessary with the wild honeybee population nearly extinct. Officially, environmental degradation and disease were the culprits for the decimation, but recently, with a quarter of all apicultural beehives dying off as well, Paul wondered if there was more to the story.

In the late summer of 1995, he was forced to deal with the problem head-on when tragedy struck his own animal companions. Normally, during that time of the year, his bees, like all honeybees, were in a frantic dash to capture the last food of the season. Making a beeline for the clover, asters, goldenrod and wild asters, they would plant themselves in the midst of the nectar-and-pollen-rich blossoms, feast and zip back to share the bounty with the colony.

But at the end of July, his beloved pollinators were no longer abuzz with activity. Though they continued to work the hive, as time passed, more and more, the bees seemed enervated. In six weeks, every honeybee in the 35-hive community was afflicted by the same debilitating condition. Invaded by Varroa mites (parasites who attach themselves to a bee's back and underside, and then drain the bodily fluids), all the bees and the hives' larvae eventually died.

As each hive fell silent, Paul too felt drained by helplessness and a heavy heart. As surely as one loved a dog or a cat, or any animal companion, he loved the bees. Stung by the loss, he recalled the story of Aristaeus, the Greek god who so bereaved his lost bees, he was willing to do anything to get them back. Understanding Aristaeus' reaction, Paul set out to figure out how he could help the honeybee. Aware of two things—the best way to fend off disease was to have a strong immune system, and the best way to achieve that was to live a life as stress free as possible—Paul began seeking a healthy solution.

Encouraged by a long-time friend familiar with the work of an animal intuitive on the West Coast, he considered calling the communicator. What attracted Sharon Callahan to him was not just her reputation for animal communication but also her knowledge of flower essences. Her connection to flowers would surely provide a natural connection to honeybees.

As his session began with Sharon, Paul told her how he'd lost his hives and how he was looking for a way to provide a healthier environment for the next families of honeybees he hoped to have on his place. After much investigation, he felt as if part of the solution would be to construct a beehive that was more analogous to those formed in nature. It would be, he believed, less stressful than today's conventional file-cabinet structures. But he added that he figured there was more than just the physical connection to being healthy. He hoped by her communicating with the bees that he was going to obtain next, he might learn about that whole ball of wax as well.

Laughing at his humor, Sharon told Paul she'd be pleased to work with the bees, if they so chose. As the animal intuitive blended with the honeybees—with their collective voice, they communicated for all bees, past, present and future—she noticed how the communication had its own distinct sweet flavor. Whispering with words delivered so softly she had to strain to decipher them, the creatures, just as they lived their lives in community, spoke as one. Their energy, she explained to Paul, was like the whirring hum of their wings, harmoniously high pitched and ethereal.

Relaying to Sharon that she was to assure Paul he was on the right track with the new beehive plans, the honeybees transmitted what would help them thrive. They said Paul was right about stress. The less they had, the healthier they would be to do their essential work.

He was also correct about the hive. A design that returns the hive to a more natural form, like the feral, tree-based, conical shape, would be beneficial. They asked that he listen to his inner guidance for the design, for he already had an understanding of the many sides of geometry.

As for the inside of the hive, Sharon said the bees had a specific request: they wanted something naturally fibrous to attach their honeycombs to. Conventional trays have honeycomb sections that are too large. Trying to cover the extra, unnatural space not only stressed them, but also weakened their bodies, making them easy targets for deadly predators like the mite.

Sharon stopped delivering the bees' messages for a moment to ask Paul why beekeeping trays were made like that. He replied that it was not only traditional, but it was also market driven. The larger the area to attach a comb to, the more honey would be produced.

Whispering again to Sharon, the bees told the animal communicator that honey was meant to help humankind as a medicinal aid rather than just a food. With nature's flowers as its source, honey was most beneficial when used sparingly and sacredly. Overuse not only guaranteed the bees' being exploited, but it could also be viewed as a mirror to a culture's excess and greed.

As those who tended to the earth, the bees emphasized that they considered their mirroring work important. With their culture of working for the good of all in the hive, they mirrored to humankind the importance of giving over the Ego Self for the love for all. People often do this during disasters and calamities, but once life returns to the humdrum, the honeybees pointed out, people often forget to continue this generous spirit.

Paul, however, was not of this group. With his heartfelt desire to help the bees' colonies, and in return the planet's welfare, he understood his animal companions' reflective message about unconditional giving and love. Their human friend, the bees conveyed to Sharon, with his loving willingness to create a comfortable, efficient home and workplace for them, reflected a bright example of this life-sustaining approach. It was a soul connection that proclaimed a higher awareness of all creatures.

Noting that the honeybees' energy hummed even more intensely, Sharon continued to listen to their transmission to Paul. They next spoke of the sacred. Sacredness, or the art of honoring all, they communicated, was the true wax to keeping life stuck together. Whether in relationship to the planet or its creatures, every being should treat another sacredly. For honoring all with respect and love is pure honey to the soul.

As the bees' collective voice ebbed, ending the communiqué, Sharon shared with Paul her own appreciation for these benevolent animals. Bees, as pollinators, hold the vibration of love on earth, for their existence is based on ensuring life for the whole. But we as humans must love them back or they will wither away, just as their bodies do when mites drain their very life force. This lack of love, she felt, was instrumental in the species' dying off today.

Replying that he understood that, Paul thanked her for serving as a conduit to his animal companions. Before he hung up, he asked if she had any flower essences for him to use when he was ready to house colonies in their new hives. After all, bees, of all animals, understood and responded well to the good energy of flowers! She agreed to send him Marsh marigold, a flower that addressed sacred purposes and strong communication between species

In the next several months, Paul focused on the design and construction of a new beehive. One day, as he sketched a possible design, he recalled his research on sacred geometry, geometrical archetypes and their vibrational resonances. Of the shapes, the five platonic solids held his attention. To the early Greeks, these solids symbolized fire, earth, air, water and spirit. The first four were indicative of the planet's physical nature. But the latter, representing spirit, seemed closest to the next realm of consciousness, a realm the honeybees were most likely familiar with. The shape was the dodecahedron, a 12-sided figure, with each side in the shape of a pentagon. With a bit of tweaking, Paul believed the perfect construct for his bees lay in his hands.

Retaining the spherical shape of the bottom half of the dodecahedron, he extended the lines of the upper half to form a five-sided top. The shape resembled a teardrop. (How appropriate, Paul thought. In Egyptian mythology, bees were the tears of the sun god Ra.) The conical shape would assist the honeybees with their honeycombs. Now, not only did their cells not have to fit the square corner mold, but also when the worker bees, suspended in great chains, hung on to one another to create the cells, positioning would be less stressful.

For the inside of the beehive, Paul, as the bees had requested, sought a natural, fibrous material. He finally located repellent-free, rice stalk squares that were sold as mats for making a household rug. In the hive, their fibrous consistency would offer sound support for honey-comb construction.

Once Paul completed the initial conical hive and spring had arrived, it was time to introduce the bees he had purchased recently to the new hive. Before transferring the bees, he sprayed a dilution of the flower essences directly onto the bees, then into the new hive's water tray. Removing the queen with a rubber spatula, Paul walked to the new structure with the matriarch and her colony of 40,000 bees swarming around her. As he shook the swarm onto the spherical hive, some of the bees headed for the nearby trees. Following them, he found many hanging onto a tree branch. Before long, all of the colony were out of the experimental hive.

Thinking they didn't like their new home, he was at first crestfallen. But when he walked back to the hive, most followed and entered in. Those remaining in the tree, however, couldn't be coaxed to leave. Finally realizing that the bees were trying to communicate vital information to him, he stood still for a moment and listened to their excited, yet happy hum. There was no doubt the creatures liked the new hive; most inside were settling in. As for the tree huggers, maybe they were just trying to show him where they wanted that brand new house. Moving the beehive under the tree, he watched them join the others in their family. Soon all the bees were busy domesticating their hive. Checking on them daily, he continued to find them peacefully productive.

On the phone with Sharon for his scheduled reading a month later, Paul described the new beehive and the bees' reactions to it. He felt they were happy with the teardrop design but wanted to know for sure if it was truly to the bees' liking. He asked the animal intuitive to communicate with them.

As she slipped into the bees' realm, they conferred to her that they were indeed pleased with the sacred conical beehive and that they were looking forward to Paul's next novel plan. When Sharon queried Paul on this, he explained that he had purchased 200 acres of cropland to form a bee sanctuary. Using 12 of the dodecahedron beehives and 12 conventional hives, his plan was to do a controlled study on the productivity of the two residences. During that time, he hoped to keep talking to the bees through Sharon. She and they assured him they'd be there.

As the session wound down, Sharon asked Paul if he would consider helping out a friend of hers who wanted to bring honeybees onto her property. Adele's intention was to have them around not to harvest their honey, but to enjoy their uplifting energy. Agreeing to send his teardrop hive plans to Adele's carpenter, Paul said he'd be willing to talk Adele through the transfer process once the hive was ready and the bees were acquired.

That November, with three pounds of bees from an organic farm, Adele prepared to place her new animal companions in their hives. Standing on a hill 50 feet from her home, she held her cell phone to her ear. Connected to Paul, she followed his step-by-step instructions from his place 3,000 miles away. In short order, Adele had moved, without resistance, the new residents. Homesteading the teardrop hives, the bees were already busy with their various jobs. The transfer was a success.

Beside her, Sharon tuned into the bees, confirming their satisfaction. As the animal intuitive assured Adele that all was well, she asked her to congratulate Paul on his design and on his motives. Magnanimous in spirit, they were much like the bees' own caring motives: selfless, loving and pure.

Walking down the hill with her friend Adele, she recalled a passage from one of her most treasured books of junior high school, J. Alan Boone's *Kinship with Life*. Its message hummed in rich synchronicity with the bees' purpose here on Adele's land and everywhere: "Accompanying each one of those lessons was the indirect but important reminder that he and almost all other animals, except those spoiled by human association, always live out from a pure heart, that is from, pure motives."

RON BRELAND

The Apis mellifera and their dodecahedron hives.

11

FOLLOWING THE HEART'S LEAD

He wouldn't fight and be fierce no matter what
they did. He just sat and smelled. And the
Banderilleros were mad and the Picadores were
madder and the Matador was so mad he cried
because he couldn't show off with his cape and
sword. So they had to take Ferdinand home.
And for all I know he is sitting there still,
under his favorite tree, smelling the flowers just
quietly. He is very happy.

The Story of Ferdinand, Munro Leaf

He was 12 years old today, and, as he strolled around the store with Barbara and Warren, he was soaring with delight. Directing them with a very vocal "over there, over there" to the various displays full of toys and goodies, he'd invariably approach each section with an ardent "wow."

After much deliberation, Jupiter settled on an edible puzzle, an intricately nut-stuffed brainteaser; bird "gum," a chew of vegetable-tanned strips of leather; and for shredding, a woven palm-frond delight.

As the store owner bagged the treats, she confided to the 18 1/2–ounce Red-fronted Macaw parrot that he was the only bird she'd let shop in her place uncaged or untethered. Jupiter replied with his customary "good job, good work" and "thank you," enchanting the woman and everyone else in the store.

Handing the cashier her credit card, Barbara looked over at her husband. Warren's eyes, much like the gentle Northwest rain that fell outside, were misty. Swiftly wiping the wetness from her own eyes, Barbara knew he was feeling more than pride, for she too was feeling a gumbo of emotions. The mixture—happiness, with nostalgia and a twist of melancholy—had been simmering in their hearts for a few weeks now.

But in the avian heart, she suspected, another emotion was bubbling as well: sheer excitement. An anticipation that went beyond waiting to play with birthday gifts, the charge was connected to another expectation that would soon take flight.

Back at the house as Jupiter perched on his ring and Marie (the African Gray) perched on hers, Warren and Barbara joined the parrots in the den. With its tree-scene wallpaper, two airy cages and array of bird equipment on the linoleum-tiled rookery side, and its comfy couch, lamp and reading table on the carpeted side, the space was truly a family room.

In a few days, however, the family would change in number. The beloved Macaw would be leaving for a bird sanctuary several states away. It had been a painful decision, but one that the Washington state couple knew they had to make—not for their own desires, for they'd always assumed that Jupiter would be with them for decades, but for the unconfined love they shared for their animal companion.

More than once, Warren and Barbara had discussed how this was like having one's child leave the nest for college. Though you knew it was timely and for the child's best interests, that didn't alter the heartache.

With his left arm propped up on the chair and his hand extended, Warren sat in his recliner, holding Jupiter in his palm. Scratching the back of the parrot's head (his ear), Warren grinned as he watched Jupiter close his eyes and open his mouth in ecstasy. When the man finished petting his animal companion, the bird gave him his customary vocal "good job" evaluation.

Going over her list of preps for Jupiter's departure, Barbara looked up at the two. As the predominant caregiver of Jupiter, she had become wonderfully close to the bird. But she couldn't deny that he and Warren had a special rapport as well.

She was proud of her husband. Growing up on a chicken farm, he had known birds only as a source for food or income. To consider that they had feelings, thoughts and personalities never occurred to him. When she and Warren contemplated having parrots as animal companions, after the death of a treasured dog, she recalled how Warren hesitated. An acquaintance had said parrots were just small green chickens. The idea of coming home from work to roost with those creatures seemed not only unsettling, but also a bit ironic to him. But, in time, he would be the wiser for truly getting to know these birds.

An urban woman, Barbara had a different perspective on animals. As animal companions, with their own preferences and emotions, she believed their service was beyond providing foodstuffs and labor. Their biggest gift was to serve as partners to their human companions and maybe even shed some lessons along the way. For she had to admit she was working on a big one right now with Jupiter.

Leaning back in her chair, she thought back to when the multi-colored Macaw first flew into her heart. She'd heard about Jupiter through a friend who knew a breeder of rare parrots. When she went to see the man, she was told the bird was not for sale as a pet. Insisting that she wasn't so much interested in having him as a pet in the caged way most people think about birds, but as a companion, she tried to convince him to let the Macaw go with her. She left that afternoon empty handed, and she left her heart with the tiny red-fronted bird whose feathers also sported brilliant greens, yellows, blues, blacks and oranges.

Over the next several months, while she studied up on the parrot species, she also pecked away at Jupiter's resistant owner. Finally, the breeder relinquished.

Hatched from a cold egg and raised in an incubator, Jupiter had never known another Red-fronted Macaw. But to Barbara, who knew she could be a close second to a loving mother figure, that was the least of her worries. Teaching the bird to perch was her first lofty challenge.

Initially, she thought Jupiter had neurological damage from birth. But she soon realized that with having been kept on a wire before she got him, Jupiter had no concept of perching on a rod. Instead of having his toes forward and back around the perch, he would put all his toes forward and simply hawk forward, creating a recipe for inevitable falls. With a trampoline built under his ring stand and three years of perching exercises from Barbara, along with her vocal reminders to watch his feet, Jupiter eventually got a grip on the art of avian roosting.

But soon another kind of tumble put him in a tailspin. An acute observer of her animal companion, Barbara began noticing that the Macaw was persistently chewing his feet, as if to quell a constant itchiness.

At the animal clinic, after blood and fecal tests, the vet diagnosed the problem as yeast. Pointing out that Jupiter's species normally lives in a dry section of Brazil, the veterinarian said that the rainy Northwest, with its ongoing dampness, along with the parrot's diet, was aiding the growth of the yeast infection. Barbara went to work on both.

Installing a dehumidifier in the house helped with the wet atmosphere. Dietary changes demanded more time and trials, but eventually she successfully established a working nonfruit formula for Jupiter that included 50 percent vegetables and greens; 40 percent nonwheat cereals and grains, such as amaranth, millet, quinoa, brown rice and oats; and 10 percent legumes. Spirilina and garlic, along with a liquid calcium/magnesium supplement, rounded off the diet.

In time, the Macaw no longer clawed his feet. His energy level increased as well, though his outgoing personality never waned at all, Barbara noticed with humor, when he was struggling with the candida. Always the commentator, Jupiter was not one to miss a chance to offer vocal reports on everything that was going on around the house, including the yard. No one could walk near the place without Jupiter's announcement that someone was there.

His assistance went beyond playing security guard. Picking up dirty clothes from the basket on the nearby table as Barbara was doing and placing them in the washing machine, Jupiter helped with the laundry. Before she started the machine and let the water fill the tub, however, he'd secure the clothes in place by lying on top of them and proclaiming "there, we did it." It was an amusing ritual that could not be broken.

There was no doubt about it, she thought as she looked at Jupiter: the bird sitting across from her could make her laugh. Putting tomatoes, one of his favorite foods, in his dish one day, Barbara was surprised to hear him announce that he didn't like those. She retorted that yes, he did. A 30-second pause filled the moment. Leaning his head to his right, piercing Barbara with his shrewd eyes, he then cackled. Realizing that she had been on the receiving end of one of Jupiter's jokes, she joined in on his infectious laughter.

Over the years, Barbara observed over and over again that the parrot's clever sense of humor and unending quest for intellectual stimulation could never be grounded. Not long ago, Jupiter had brought an old children's game to life. Sitting on his ring in the living room just steps away from the kitchen, he watched Barbara go to the refrigerator. Opening the door, Barbara searched for a snack. Thinking she was going to tease him, she peeked around the door and gave him a vocal peek-a-boo. Stone-faced, Jupiter did nothing. The next morning, as she prepared her breakfast, she opened the refrigerator door. With a bowl of oats in one hand and some yogurt in the other, she used her hips to push the door closed. As it brushed by her face, she looked up to see Jupiter leaning around the living room corner toward her. The Red-fronted Macaw exclaimed a sonorous "peek."

The memory still made her laugh. Giggling aloud, Barbara interrupted the boys. When Warren asked what had her so tickled, she relayed the story of the peek-a-boo exchange. Smiling, he said it was those things he'd miss the most. Not that Marie, their sweet bird whom Jupiter had welcomed when she was introduced into the family four years ago, wasn't special. Turning to the African Gray, Warren rubbed her and told her so. "But," the man acknowledged with a catch in his voice, "well, Jupe-guy was one unique bird." Even Marie adored him. Marie confirmed the statement with a "Jupe good boy."

Stroking Jupiter's neck once more, Warren told his wife and his "kids" he was going to miss their morning times together. Starting the day with the parrots' "good morning" and feeding them their cereal, the day just seemed to get off to a better start for him. And with the birds' ability to eat and talk at the same time—they would rate the cereal "very good" as they nabbed the grain with their beaks—their breakfasts together had always been a social treat.

Though Warren admitted that Sundays with his buddy Jupiter had their own savory flavor too. After breakfast, shower time took center stage. Positioned in Warren's hand, Jupiter would half spread his wings and preen under the misty water. After that, Warren would place the Macaw on the PVC pipe and suction cup stand he had constructed for his animal companion. By bouncing the spray off his shoulder onto the laughing bird, Warren showered a happy Jupe-guy with the warm water.

Commenting on everything from the pleasure of the falling water ("whee") to Warren's handling of the bath ("good work, War"), the Macaw would speak with the command and clarity of a precocious preschool child.

Besides the ecstasies of life, Jupiter also felt and shared in the household's distressing moments. With his genetics, that was a natural. Parrots, being flock animals (as opposed to pack animals who join together for defense or attack), are keen on being a big part of the family environment. Warren had seen that with his wife and the sympathetic parrot. More than once, when Barbara was sad, or the stress of her career was twisting her into knots, the parrot would rub his beak across his human companion's head, consoling her with "there, there."

Nodding, Barbara reminded Warren that was how they had come to know Sharon Callahan, the animal intuitive. During one of the Macaw's empathetic periods, Jupiter's concern for her had become so consuming that it began to leak into his own well-being, and his health began to decline.

Communicating with the Macaw, the animal intuitive had explained that Jupiter was mirroring Barbara's stress. Assuring the bird that it wasn't his job to take her under his wing to his detriment, Barbara, also confronting her own emotional issues, watched the bird's health improve with time. Life in the household seemed to be flying high. But Jupiter's recent, puzzling behaviors netted the bird and his human family tonight's session with Sharon.

Although Jupiter could always be counted on to speak his mind, he had never been the negative one. Only rarely did he express his displeasure with loud, irritable squawking. But over the past two years, his high-pitched requests, most notably for her time, had steadily increased. Never one to just perch and wait for something to intrigue him, Jupiter needed constant stimulation. In frustration, every now and then, he'd even bite.

Even his affection for certain TV programs—old TV comedies, like Red Skeleton in his clown getup or bird documentaries on the *Animal Planet*, or easy listening music on the radio—could appease him only for so long.

Concerned about her animal companion, Barbara took the parrot to the vet. When he found no physical ailments, Barbara knew she had to look beyond the physical. Dealing with acting-out Macaws, with their high intelligence and emotional sensitivity, she read, was often like dealing with a child who had a behavior problem: there was usually something deeper going on than the obvious.

At home, Barbara put a restless Jupiter on his ring stand and left the room to finish some bookkeeping tasks. But the Macaw wanted her to stay to entertain, as well as challenge, him in conversation and play. With each step she took out of the room, he screamed louder, "Barb, it hurt, it hurt; do good job here." Walking over to him, she stoked his head and told him she loved him, but she couldn't be with him all the time. With his head bowed, Jupiter nodded, then leaned his beak back and squawked. Barbara sighed. Deciding she'd seek the help of Sharon once more, she scheduled an appointment.

On the phone with the animal communicator, Barbara began the session by describing Jupiter's behaviors. She then asked Sharon to find out why her animal companion seemed so distraught. Was he not feeling well, or, as she suspected and feared, was the sharp bird just dulled by life?

Merging with Jupiter, Sharon quickly communicated with the Macaw via thought transfers. Just as she'd been when she'd spoken with him months before, Sharon was smitten by the bird's intelligence. She remarked to Barbara that it was like talking to a five year old. But that wasn't unusual when communicating with these kinds of birds, she told her client. Each time she had a reading with a parrot, the bird's mental aptitude was a prominent characteristic of the conversation.

Yet, she had seen in her work that their innate cleverness could also work against these flock animals. Gregarious creatures, they needed much stimulation, both from their own kind and their caregivers. They did not do well when they were treated like just a simple animal with feathers or, more tragically, when they were placed in a corner like an object that was noticed only when the person was inclined to. Eventually the lack of attention caused them to react like any neglected being: they would withdraw, become ill or act out.

Jupiter had acted out, not because Barbara had ignored or mistreated him, but because the bright Macaw, like a gifted youngster, just needed more from his environment. Communicating to Sharon, he wanted to make sure Barbara understood that he appreciated his family of human companions and his friend Marie very much. All had treated him with respect and kindness, and he was conflicted by the hurt he may cause them with the request he was about to make. But he had to follow where his heart was leading him.

That direction was back to a family that he felt in his core being and that he'd only seen on TV but had never known. Quite simply, he relayed to the animal intuitive, he wanted to be around those of his own kind, to soar with other Red-fronted Macaws in play, feelings and thought.

As she relayed this heart-wrenching appeal from Jupiter, Sharon noted to Barbara that Jupiter's concern for his current companions was uniquely sincere. Even more so because he was a bird.

"Birds," she explained, "unlike dogs and cats who have a long history of relationships with people, truly do have a bird's-eye view of feelings. That is, they have a certain detachment that can allow them to see the picture of things from an *emotional above*. Not that they don't have deep feelings or that they don't like the physical expression of such inner sentiments that is, touch, they do. But, they are not drenched in all-consuming human emotions."

For Barbara, her Jupiter's request to leave hit her like a truckload of basalt rock from the nearby Cascade Mountains. For 12 years, Jupiter had been with her and Warren in a home where she had provided the utmost in care and love. He was their colorful, quick-witted boy, the joy of their home. Yet, she confessed to Sharon, she couldn't deny that it came as no surprise that he needed more out of life than they all could give him. But dealing with the reality of his leaving was not an easy idea to swallow.

Barbara asked the animal communicator where Jupiter could possibly go. Sharon said there were reputable bird sanctuaries in the country that she might research. Jupiter communicated that he knew Barbara would find the best one for him.

As the session ended, a still-shaken Barbara pitched one more question. Remembering that Sharon had told her before that animals often mirror their human partners, she wanted to know what Jupiter could possibly be mirroring to her.

Sharon responded that just as Jupiter was seeking to follow his heart's desire, Barbara must also be brave enough to peck through her fears to follow what her heart was telling her. When Barbara countered that her heart was aching and not eager to let Jupiter go, Sharon asked that she look beyond the emotions of it all and peer into the chambers of her real heart, her soul, to embrace the message there.

Over the next few days, Barbara mulled over this turn of events. In time, she found herself slowly turning her fear of loss of control over Jupiter's care (she'd always prided herself on keeping the fragile bird healthy), as well as her fear of not having his endearing physical presence with her, into a genuine acceptance of his request. Her lesson, she realized, was to follow her heart by listening to her inner voice that reminded her that sometimes she had to let go to be able to hold on. By letting go, she was not only allowing the best to be, but she was allowing Jupiter to be the best of who he was: an intelligent, Red-fronted Macaw who ached to flock with his own. Wasn't that what real love was, after all?

Like her, Warren was initially incredulous that Jupe-boy would want to leave their loving home, but he also understood that he and his wife could not challenge the mentally adroit bird 24/7. They were not Macaws, and the parrot deserved to know his genetic family.

Searching the Internet, Barbara began a quest to locate the best sanctuary for their animal companion. After much research and a trip to the private reserve, she opted for a place near the Rocky Mountains.

When she next spoke to Sharon for a session with Jupiter before the move, she detailed her preparations for the trip. She also wanted to know if Jupiter had any concerns about the transition.

Merging with Jupiter's thoughts, Sharon indicated that the bird had no major questions to ask because Barbara had done such a good job of showing him the place through pictures, a video and conversation. Yet, he admitted to Sharon that he was a little nervous going to a new place. But even more, he was excited. He was following his heart's lead.

His only concern now was Warren and Barbara. He wanted to make sure they were going to be okay when he was gone. He also wanted to remind his human friends that he would let them know how it was there; he'd give complete reports through Barbara's sessions with Sharon.

Laughing, Barbara and Sharon agreed that Jupiter would indeed be a good reporter, as he was an avid talker, even one known to do a bit of tattling.

The animal intuitive also assured the two that she would be pleased to assist them during the transfer stage. In fact, she'd found in her work that one of the biggest values of an animal communication session is having a dialogue between human and animal companions when an animal has to be relocated or must change caregivers for one reason or another. "After the relocation," Sharon added, "the sessions between the two parties seem even more relevant."

Over the next three months, relieved that Sharon would continue to communicate with Jupiter, Barbara put the plans for the move into action. When the day arrived to make the long drive to the sanctuary, Barbara and Warren packed the car and rental trailer with all the belongings Jupiter had selected, as well as a six-month supply of the special-diet foods she'd prepared for him.

Along the way, Warren pointed out things for Jupe-boy to see. With all these first-time sights, the bird, ever eager for more, gushed so many "wows" that Warren and Barbara found themselves caught up in their Macaw's enthusiasm.

But it was when Jupiter was actually on the sanctuary grounds that he truly expressed his bursting joy. As Barbara assisted the staff with Jupiter's things and his food requirements, Warren, with Jupe-boy in his cage, gave the parrot a tour of the grounds. The animated bird cackled with glee at the horses, llamas and mules on the farm; he exclaimed, "wow, look at that" as his human companion placed him on a rock lookout to view the mountains and surrounding valleys. He offered a "good work" when Warren showed him inside his living quarters, demonstrating what door he would use to go in and out of the building.

But the pièce de résistance was what the new resident saw when Warren actually stepped outside into the backyard aviary: peppering the area, over 100 birds of varying species, most of whom had been rescued, met his eyes. For once, Jupiter, with his mouth agape and his eyelids wide open, said nothing. Rotating his head like an oscillating fan in slow motion, he captured each section of the yard with an unblinking stare.

As the man and the parrot stood by the door surveying the scene, the sun began to drop behind the building, and the staff began to collect the birds to return them to their cages inside for the night.

One by one, each perched on a caretaker's arm, the cockatoos, amazons, African Grays, cockatiels and even small birds, such as finches, paraded past Jupiter. But it was the last two feathered creatures who enraptured the new boy at the sanctuary.

Coming toward him and Warren was a blaze of red, surrounded by vibrant greens, yellows, blues, blacks and oranges. No longer would he need a mirror to see a Red-fronted Macaw; here in front of him, and followed by a second, was one in living color.

As Jupiter gazed at the two parrots filing past him, Barbara joined the boys. She and Warren exchanged proud, teary-eyed glances as they asked their animal companion what he thought about it all. With his eyes glued to the Macaws until the birds disappeared into the building, Jupe-boy answered with a visceral "good job, good job, Bar, good job, War, thank you."

As promised, Jupiter continued to communicate with Barbara and Warren through Sharon in the days that followed his entrance into the bird sanctuary. He reported he was getting accustomed to his new routine; he liked the human caregivers there and, of course, he was still thrilled at being with his own kind. Not that he didn't miss everyone back at his old home, he did, for he still loved them very much. Thanks to them, he was now living a life that brought him a new experience everyday and something more: his spirit soared. As he spent the last of the Indian summer days outside with his other family, viewing the colorful leaves around him and smelling the sweet air, his heart was indeed happy.

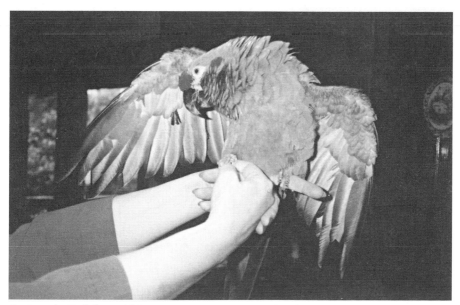

Jupiter, the Red-fronted Macaw.

Sitting at her desk one night, Sharon returned to the poignant thoughts Jupiter had sent her way. Through the bird's story, she was reminded of an important Universal Truth about finding true happiness: follow the heart's lead.

Jupiter's story also recalled a favorite book from her childhood. In *The Story of Ferdinand*, the message was the same. Though the parrot's circumstances were obviously different from the bull's, he was determined to follow his heart just as Ferdinand had done.

Opening her tattered copy of the book, she read again the familiar passage: "He wouldn't fight and be fierce no matter what they did. He just sat and smelled. And the Banderilleros were mad and the Picadores were madder and the Matador was so mad he cried because he couldn't show off with his cape and sword. So they had to take Ferdinand home. And for all I know he is sitting there still, under his favorite tree, smelling the flowers just quietly. He is very happy."

12

GOOD THOUGHTS

Jonathan Seagull discovered that boredom and
fear and anger are the reasons that a gull's life
is so short, and with these gone from his
thought, he lived a long, fine life indeed.

Jonathan Livingston Seagull, Richard Bach

Driving to her morning appointment, Diana mulled over the latest developments in her life and sighed. Leaving behind an established business, friends and family, she'd followed her physician husband to a new city, one in which she didn't feel at home.

Las Vegas was not Pasadena. Here, in this Nevada city, she felt malnourished and bare, much like the desert landscape that surrounded her. Fair-skinned and petite, she seemed to shrink under the relentless sun. She missed the familiar face of her former California home: the urban forest, the tree-lined streets, the San Gabriel Mountains and the thriving art and theatre scene.

Her grief was recently compounded when a beloved aunt, who had been a second mother to Diana, died. That heartache, along with the stress from the relocation, seemed to permeate her thoughts and her feelings. On a roller coaster, her emotions dipped with sadness and boredom, stalled with fear and frustration and rose with anger and anxiety. Even her physical body was expressing the angst. Her once-abundant, golden hair was now falling out, leaving bald patches that were becoming difficult to conceal.

As she touched one of those naked spots with her left hand, her right hand turned the steering wheel down a busy thoroughfare toward her destination. Suddenly, a panicked ragamuffin-of-a-dog streaked across the street in front of her and ran to a nearby parking lot. In a sur-real time frame, Diana's heart raced along with the frightened canine. Hoping to help, Diana quickly pulled over to the area, jumped out of the car and cornered the frenzied animal. The dog, hairless and encrusted with sores, did not run. Instead, the female lay vulnerably on her back, her scabby stomach exposed. Responding to this act of sub-mission, Diana approached and scooped up the emaciated body. With the flea-covered dog in her lap, Diana directed her car to the vet's office.

Examining the shaking creature, the doctor diagnosed the animal with a severe case of mange and malnutrition. He remarked that it was too bad, for he could see she was once a well-cared-for dog, though she'd certainly seen some rough times lately.

Diana agreed to the two-week hospital stay that it would take to treat the cockapoo. She had no doubts about that decision. Already, she felt a compelling connection to this animal, as if their meeting were no accident.

As she left the clinic, she knew whom she would call about Charli, the name she had chosen for the canine. Last year, Animal Intuitive Sharon Callahan had helped Diana make some fateful decisions when their critically ill family dog was in his last days. Now, confident of the communicator's abilities, Diana hoped that Sharon could help decipher not only Charli's life, but (and equally important) the purpose of Charli and Diana's coming together.

During the session, as Sharon merged with Charli, the dog com-municated not with images but with feelings and, occasionally, some basic thought transfers. This was not unusual for an abused animal, Sharon told Diana. Accustomed to a life that resorted to the basics for survival, battered creatures often expressed themselves in elementary ways. Later on, as the animal becomes less anxious, he or she can see the world more clearly and can use those vivid mental pictures to communicate. Charli was not there yet.

Immersed in Charli's sensory history, Sharon detailed the canine's life before Diana. A beloved animal companion to an elderly lady who had been placed in a retirement home, Charli was given to a little boy and his family. But the father didn't like the dog, so he abandoned her in the city, leaving Charli to live on the streets, homeless, ever hungry and frightened. But life took a sweet turn when she had a litter of puppies and she felt the joy of giving and receiving love again. But that too ended in tragedy. After the loss of the puppies, Charli contracted mange. The constant itching directed at the parasitic mites left her with sores and hair loss, only adding to her pain.

Yet, through the agony, Charli relayed to Sharon, she had not given up on life. Though thrown into an inhospitable environment, kicked in the gut by grief from the loss of her puppies (as well as physically by the boot of many a human) and bereft of her much-needed hair, she was dogged in her faith to stay on all fours until she had fulfilled a crucial life purpose. That purpose was Diana.

Transmitting the image of a mirror to Sharon, Charli communicated that she was in Diana's life to serve as a faithful mirror to this kind woman who had rescued her from the streets. With loving, and sometimes painfully honest reflections of her human companion's feelings, attitudes and behaviors, Charli would be a reliable looking glass. For by reflecting both the jostles of Diana's heart and the joys of her soul, Charli would help her see herself clearly, without distortion and without judgment.

Already, Sharon told Diana, the animal companion was performing this mirroring work. With the thought transfers the canine was sending to her, Sharon pointed out the obvious reflections: both Charli and Diana were experiencing great sorrow; both felt out of their element and lonely in a seemingly hostile place; and, as was physically apparent, both were losing their hair.

As Charli's story concluded, Diana confirmed that her new animal companion's evaluation of her was right on target. Yet, though she wouldn't deny there was already a profound bond between her and Charli, she wondered about the giant task the small dog had collared for herself. Sharon explained to Diana that animal companions take the role of mirroring very seriously, considering it an act of devoted service that supersedes all others.

Charli was no different, and her dedication to her human friend didn't stop there. With an unwavering belief in Diana's ability to reconnect to her core spirit, Charli would stand, sit, run and play by Diana's side to help her mend her shattered heart and move forward with courage.

"Then," the dog imaged to Sharon, "perhaps Diana's thoughts could float to the highest clouds of a positive mind set. In this space, she could breathe fully again, without the choking sighs of grief and disappointment. Taking in the peaceful air surrounding her new place, she might even find that the desert had its own sweet perfume called home."

To help both Charli and Diana adjust to new situations, as well as deal with their losses, the animal intuitive proposed a flower essence made from the yew tree. She noted that the yew, with a lifespan of thousands of years, was the epitome of spiritual resurrection and survival.

For the next nine months, with holistic veterinary care and much loving care from Diana, Charli made an impressive physical transformation. Her mangy skin was left behind, and thick, silky champagne-colored hair returned to the cockapoo. The dog, once jumpy and weak, was now a sweet-natured animal content in her new domicile.

Unveiling a natural effervescent energy, Charli began to step into a balanced world of play and proprietary joy. One of the first things Diana gave her new animal companion was a ball. Charli, who had never been given much at all during her early years, soon became attached to the ball, as if the toy gift were a symbol for being honored.

Sensing that, Diana gave her more. Whether gently carrying them, like newborn puppies, to a hiding place or roughhousing with them in quintessential dog revelry, Charli and her brightly colored balls were never far apart. Even when she generously allowed Diana's mother's dog to play with the plush circles, Charli kept a steady eye on the balls all the time, making sure no bouncers left the house.

That never failed to make Diana laugh. Walking around the pool with Charli, picking up one of the dog's balls that had rolled under a lawn chair, Diana thought how Charli wasn't the only one reflecting changes in the household. Coming home stressed from the hospital, her husband Will always welcomed the new family member to his lap. Charli's adoring eyes and caring energy would soothe yet invigorate him. Will's and Charli's routine soon became a nightly ritual.

Diana, too, was beginning to feel more trusting and lovingly proprietary about life and its gifts. Not that there wasn't more hard work ahead—her heart still ached—but she *was* coming out of her shell.

As if on cue, a glint from the water lured her to the pool's edge. Wading into the blue-green liquid, she saw a dark object about five inches long on the pool floor. It was a turtle with a hat on her green and gold striped head. Scooping up the animal, she realized the hat was an enlarged pus sac.

At the vet's office, the doctor examined the grayish black turtle with the rich, orange-bottomed shell. Besides the ear abscess that would require surgery, the veterinarian pointed out holes and heavily etched marks on the painted turtle's shell. Identifying them as dog-teeth signatures, he noted that they had come from more than one attack. That meant, he added that she'd obviously been through some ordeals. But other than those problems, the veterinarian concluded that the battered turtle appeared to be in fairly good shape. He concluded the exam by asking Diana if she knew much about turtles.

Confessing that she didn't, but it looked as if she was about to, she told the vet she was ready to take care of the creature. She'd come to realize that there were no accidents in the Universe. All things had purpose; Charli, her other animal companion, had shown her that.

To help with the turtle conundrum, Diana decided to contact Sharon. Believing that the animal intuitive was the person who could offer the most reliable clues, she looked forward to the session.

As Diana waited for her appointment to speak with Sharon Callahan about Tommi the turtle, she fortified a small pond in her home's spacious backyard. With its 50-tree garden that she and her husband had created, the land provided a buffer of green plants and water against the harsh landscape outside. Funny, she thought, how the house and the land around her, a place she resisted living in, had provided her with the most unusual rewards.

When the session arrived, Diana ignited the conversation with questions about Tommi. Where did she come from; what was her purpose in Diana's life; did she want another turtle for company?

Using sharp images, as well as crystalline thought transfers, Tommi communicated to Sharon that she'd last lived in an aquarium and had traveled a long way to walk through Diana's gate to the garden and pool. But her real place of origin was beyond that. Way beyond. She was from the stars. And she'd appreciate it if she would never be placed in an aquarium but always be allowed to be outside where she could see the stars.

The pond gave her that and something more. The rocks around it supplied her with a place to meditate with nature and the Universe.

As Diana's animal companion, her purpose was to be a special guide and friend. Along with Charli, Tommi would help lead a wounded Diana back to her own soul purpose. As a mirror and as an example, the painted turtle would not only show her the way, but also remind her to have faith in herself and the future. Hadn't faith gotten her to Diana?

As for a turtle companion, Tommi said she wanted to share the pond instead with some goldfish. Promising that she wouldn't eat them, Tommi told Sharon that she would like being around their sparkling, quick movements. "Opposites attract," she added. Sharon laughed, telling Diana that animals have a sense of humor, too. She'd seen that over and over again.

When Diana laughed, Tommi said Diana was already getting the real picture about life: it was about letting go of past abrasions and looking for the joy of the moment. The turtle acknowledged that she, too, was working on that. Though dogs had attacked her before, she was learning to be more comfortable around Charli. Not that she thought Charli would hurt her, but with her past experiences, it was a new friendship that required more tending.

Tommi ended her conversation with Sharon and Diana with a final request: more hugs. Contrary to what humans may think, reptiles have feelings (they're just not encouraged to express them), and they like being touched. As with all beings, no matter what the species, the loving energy of a hug or a gentle caress is the pinnacle of bliss in this tactile world.

Several months later, with Charli lying beside her, Diana knelt down at the pond's edge. Tommi's head, popping up from the water, was close enough for her to reach out and rub. Charli joined in with a swift lick of her own. Gently picking up the turtle, Diana placed Tommi in her arms and gave the animal companion a tour of the garden. Dashing forward, Charli was the scout.

As the sun began to dip down into the western sky, Diana returned Tommi to the pond. Sunset and sunrise were the turtle's special times. Emerging from the water and settling on a nearby rock, Tommi preferred to be alone as she meditated, seemingly returning to the stars and her spiritual home.

In time, Diana understood what this simple action was showing her. Tommi was teaching her that no matter what is going on around her, she should take time to reconnect to her soul. Stop, sit still and be in the moment with the Great Spirit. And here outside in the desert was a beautiful place to do that.

Charli was also doing her part in reflecting to Diana the value of good thoughts. Besides reminding Diana to believe in herself and have faith that the best was her birthright, the vivacious dog and her balls demonstrated to her human companion another life priority: punt worry out of bounds and just play. Fun was not just for children, it was the inherent joyful right of all beings.

A year later, Diana, Will, Charli and Tommi had settled into their lives outside Las Vegas. In Mt. Shasta, Sharon brought her file on Tommi and Charli up to date. Diana had reported that both were doing well. And since our animal companions mirror us, she laughingly added that she guessed that meant she was doing well, too. Though life was still pitching her curves, she was proud that she was now looking forward to every day with a new shiny awareness of all things.

As the animal intuitive made her notes, she thought about the cockapoo, the turtle and their purposes in Diana's life. With their mirroring, they had helped their human companion look deep inside and tap into a fundamental discovery.

That discovery reminded her of a quote from the book *Jonathan Livingston Seagull*: "Jonathan Seagull discovered that boredom and fear and anger are the reasons that a gull's life is so short, and with these gone from his thought, he lived a long, fine life indeed."

Charli, the Cockapoo.

Tommi, the Painted Turtle.

13

FRIENDSHIP

*The friendship between the boy and
the stallion was something too
much for them to understand.*

The Black Stallion, Walter Farley

*K*yle stepped back to cast a critical eye on the results of his latest efforts. The two-level houses for the animal companions were almost complete. Composed of glass, with the sides offering ample ventilation holes, the houses' upper story was framed by resin-free redwood. Offering light, the 35-gallon space was truly a room with a view.

The bottom story, a secluded bedroom tendering security for burrowing, hibernating or just getting away from it all, was a plastic drawer box, shuttered by wood to deter any light. The blackness afforded the animal a canopy of protection, while the plastic facilitated cleaning the aspen bedding. With a depth three times the thickness of the animal's height, the recycled paper bedding would line both floors of the house.

All that the 25-year-old southern California resident had left to do now was the electrical: heat pads for under the houses and heat lamps for over them, along with a light dimmer and a thermometer. All this would help keep the ambient temperature between 72 and 82 degrees. One thing about reptiles, Kyle knew from experience, was proper temperature maintenance is a top priority.

With thermal-regulating body temperatures, snakes can feel their homes cool long before humans can. With their poikilothermal bodies, bodies that reflect their external environment (*cold blooded,* Kyle felt, was not only inaccurate, but it also held a negative connotation that snakes were mindless and cruel), these animals don't seek the sun for light but for warmth.

The new condominiums also addressed not only his, but his wife Ariel's animal companions' needs in another way. Highly sensitive to temperature, touch and movement, snakes could easily be stressed by any unfamiliar surroundings and vibrations. Having a buffer to the world, a compact and secure refuge that offered them quiet, comfort and enclosed security, was imperative.

Though pleased with the terrariums, Kyle knew the best critique would come from a prospective resident. With Saratoga wrapped around his arm, Kyle supported the three-foot-long Goin's King snake as he introduced her to her future home. Encouraging her to give the new digs a test run, Kyle held on to her rear section assuredly as she inched into the space.

An explorer, Saratoga, regal in her skin of black-outlined crimson saddles and cream-colored bands, enjoyed occasional field trips. Watched over by her human companions, she'd swim with the fish in the oaken-barrel pond; slide along the mysterious branches of the bamboo tree on the patio; or, joining Kyle or Ariel during their card games, glide among them, looking for new burrowing adventures.

Today was no different. Flashing her tongue, she tasted the air. From smells to heat detection, Saratoga's vigilant sensory organ retrieved vital information about her environment. Though she had no ears and the eyes on either side of her head provided unreliable eyesight, her adeptness at sensing movement and vibrations was superior. With an undulating crawl around the premises, Saratoga surveyed her new condo with her reliable radar and her unending curiosity in full play.

Watching his beloved friend, Kyle recalled the first time he connected to a snake. When he was five, his dad had brought home a Gopher snake. Found by gardeners at the resort where his father worked, the serpent was about to be destroyed when Kyle's dad intervened. Volunteering to remove the hapless animal from the premises, his dad delivered the docile snake to Kyle. Enamored with the creamy-yellow creature, peppered with brown-black blotches, Kyle not only named him Honker Tree but also dedicated himself to tending to him.

Over the years, he'd learned much about the physical idiosyncrasies and needs of these amazing creatures. But, even more significantly, he'd learned that snakes were sensitive and affectionate beings, with distinct personalities, who were too often misunderstood and needlessly feared. For, like cats, dogs or any other animal companion, reptiles responded best to their human partners when treated with respect, intelligence and genuine caring.

Yet the friendship between Kyle and the reptiles was often not understood by everyone. Perhaps the animal's constant portrayal as being evil—from its role as the tempter in the biblical story of Adam and Eve, to the snake-in-the-grass bad guy in cartoons and movies—was the reason. Or maybe, he thought, it was people's fear of poisonous snakes, even though only 15 percent of all snakes in the country were poisonous. But both of these trepidations, Kyle felt, could be deleted by getting to know these fascinating creatures as he had done. Now he seemed to not only understand them, but also to identify with them.

Though he had a few close buddies and a gregarious bride (who was a magnet for drawing new and old friends into their home), he, like the snake sequestered under a favorite rock or log, could be content away from the crowds. Whether surfing, scuba diving, fishing or searching for precious stones in the nearby Mojave Desert, he was most relaxed when the stimuli around him did not encircle and grab him, like a Red-tail hawk preying on an unsheltered snake.

Aware that Saratoga was now tiring, he lifted her onto his shoulders and returned her to her current home. Peering into a hollow-log section in a nearby snake house, Kyle looked in on Killer. Burrowed in, the Honduran Milk snake appeared as only a slight lump in the shadowed bedding. Easily excited by strange surroundings, Killer would not be asked today to try out his nearly completed new home.

Smiling, Kyle remembered how Killer acquired his name. He and Ariel first saw the vibrant tangerine-colored creature with his black and yellow-orange bands at a reptile show nearly three years ago. Recently hatched, the snake appeared edgy and unsure of his surroundings. Drawn to him, Kyle asked the exhibitor if he could hold the nervous male. Wanting to reassure him, Kyle handled the tense, hissing snake with gentle, nonthreatening movements. Aware that the exposed animal sought the serenity of a warm and tight place, Kyle placed him near his fleece collar. Settling inside the jacket fold, he calmed down. Already the two were intertwined.

When Ariel reached for the little ophidian minutes later, however, the reptile's insecurity resurfaced. Though unafraid of serpents, Ariel was still learning how to handle them with confidence. Attempting to make sure she had the tangerine snake securely on her arm, she held on tightly to the animal. Too tightly. The frightened snake reacted with an instinctive oral pinch. Recalling that snakes associate intense gripping with being captured, Ariel released her grip. When they both relaxed moments later, Kyle told Ariel facetiously that he had the perfect name for this little one who was coming home with him: Killer.

Turning away from Killer's snake house, Kyle glanced over at the two empty houses in the corner of the study where Fink, his animal companion, and Flip, Ariel's, once burrowed. Both were missing.

With her coral-dusted, dark-yellow body wrapped in red saddles, Fink was a Thayer's King snake. Intimately close, Kyle and Fink had honed a keen relationship two years ago when Kyle treated his snake friend for a respiratory infection. Treatment required that he inject antibiotics into Fink's lower left muscle. Associating a sharp prick with being attacked by a predator's teeth or claws, snakes have a natural aversion to needles. Yet Fink, sensing that Kyle meant no harm, never tried to bite or wiggle away from the injections.

Fink was also very intelligent. Labeled the family escape artist, she'd twice managed to slide her terrarium top open with her nose and slip out. Fink's destination, however, was always the same: Kyle's clothes drawer, where she'd snuggle in the darkness of her human companion's T-shirts. Except this time Fink had not sought the seclusion of the drawer.

Flip turned up missing a week after Fink. Ariel's first snake companion, the sleek, energetic creature was a Baird's Rat snake. Gray and graceful, with skin like silk, he reminded her of a dolphin. But she was happy he was a snake. For though she'd grown up with cats and dogs, and loved all animals, she'd learned to appreciate the reptile's minimalist ways. With a snake, one had to be quiet to hear him. Since the creature spoke with no external sounds, that meant listening to his internal messages, his thoughts. It was a communicative method that helped her to be more focused on life's more subtle forces. It also created a sweet closeness between human and reptile.

In her San Francisco apartment before she and Kyle married, Ariel had come to rely on Flip's friendship. From the beginning, when she'd come home from her work, one of her first actions would be to take Flip out of his terrarium to be with her. Calling him her boy, she'd tell him about her day. As always, the ground snake, laced around her arm for physical support, would, in turn, give his human companion unconditional emotional support. Though he could not hear Ariel's words, he could feel their vibrational tone and would "listen" attentively to her stories. In time, as Kyle had predicted when he took her to purchase Flip, the two became tight friends. Or as she'd often say facetiously to friends with a grin, they had become wrapped up in each other.

But Flip's, as well as Fink's, disappearance was no laughing matter for the couple. Dedicated to taking top-notch care of their animal friends, Kyle and Ariel found the situation painful and puzzling. Over and over they asked how and why had their snake companions left.

Tonight, they hoped to find out. With a referral from the family veterinarian, they had an appointment to speak to Sharon Callahan, an animal communicator in Mt. Shasta. They would also seek a reading on Saratoga and Killer.

On the phone with Sharon, Kyle supplied a succinct background on why he and Ariel were calling about their four animal companions. After he finished, Sharon asked him why he had such an affinity for snakes. He replied that he felt a friendship with serpents for many reasons. Unlike a dog, who was more often friendly and trusting upfront, with a snake, it was all about developing trust on an incremental basis. You had to earn it. Kyle told Sharon that kind of behavior reminded him of himself, as he tended to keep people at arm's length at first, taking a long time to trust them completely.

But there was something else he felt about snakes, he added. He had to give the creature a lot of credit. With a history of being not only overly scrutinized and misunderstood but also feared and rejected, here was an animal who was willing to take a chance and be your intimate friend. That kind of friendship was something he admired.

But that made it even harder to think about his buddy Fink. Wondering if he'd done something to cause the snake's exodus, he admitted that he was worried about his animal friend. Was she hungry, cold—or worse—dead?

Before connecting to the snake, the animal intuitive explained to Kyle that our animal companions' actions often mean more than the obvious. Sometimes, they serve as mirrors, reflecting not only our brightest assets, but also our most shadowed angst. Both reflections offer a sacred insight into ourselves.

Merging with Fink, the animal intuitive could easily perceive the world as Fink did. That reality, Sharon told Kyle, was in some ways a dichotomy. On one hand, Fink was quick to detect both the physical and nonphysical vibrations emanating from her environment. On the other, she, like most snakes when not overly stimulated by predators or unfamiliar human encroachment, didn't pay much attention to the particulars of her surroundings. However, that natural disinterest had contributed to her current predicament.

Using thought transfer, Fink communicated that she'd gotten out of her terrarium because she just wanted to move around a bit and was going to return to her home to snuggle in. But in her wanderings, she'd found herself unable to get back to her house or to the security of Kyle's chest of drawers. Now, with the cool December days and nights, she was settled under some wood and dust and was entering the initial stages of hibernation.

In a hesitant, hurt voice, Kyle asked if Fink had left for other reasons. Was he unhappy with Kyle, or had Kyle done something wrong?

Answering with an emphatic "no," Sharon relayed Fink's response to Kyle. One thing she did want her human companion to understand was how much she appreciated Kyle's care, from nursing her back to health to tending to her daily needs.

But there was a part of her now that needed to be free, to go beyond the secure, no matter what the consequences. Even if it meant, as had happened, that she found herself in a place where she couldn't get back to her home just now. But it was meeting the challenge of the unknown that was also significant. Not just for herself, but for Kyle as well. For, as Kyle's sacred companion, it was her job to remind her human friend who Kyle really was: a worthy and beautiful being of the Universe. As a creature so many considered worthless and ugly, Fink said she understood the importance of this task.

But, she said to Sharon, her responsibility didn't stop there. As a mirror to Kyle's soul, she also wanted to remind Kyle to experience the world with more than his eyes by tuning in to the vibrations of his heart. Aware that Kyle was often content to stay in his secure environment, reluctant to seek the company of new people and opportunities, Fink hoped her own big decision to leave the comfort of home in search of life's other bounties, as well as surprises, would only serve as an example of trusting that inner guidance. By living close, but yet separate from her old home place, she also hoped that Kyle could see that life need not be black and white. It could be a positive compromise. He could move in his life and have all the solitude he needs; he could treasure his individuality yet still be interactive with society.

As a contemplative silence filled the other end of the phone line, Sharon respectfully waited. When Kyle spoke again, he said he had only one other question to ask Fink. Would she be coming back home? Transferring again her thoughts to Sharon, Fink said she wasn't sure if she'd be returning. She'd make her decision in the spring when her body could easily maneuver in her surroundings. But, either way, Kyle was to remember that he was never far away from her in spirit.

Kyle then asked about Killer. As she merged with the Milk snake, the animal intuitive noted that, of all the snakes in the couple's home, Killer offered the clearest mirror of his human companion: an intelligent, reserved being who stood back and took account of events from the periphery. Yet Killer, like Kyle, didn't miss a thing, though he never made an overt to-do about any of those observations.

Killer agreed. As Kyle's looking glass, he said his moods and actions were also reliable barometers of Kyle's own, portraying what Kyle was going through at the moment, especially when Kyle was worried or stressed. As his animal companion, that was his job. He took it very seriously, and he had no plans to leave it behind.

Telling Sharon that he and Ariel would talk to her about Saratoga together, Kyle said Ariel wanted to first ask about Flip. On the phone with the animal communicator, Ariel asked if she'd connect with Flip to find out where he might be and why he left. She really missed her baby, whom she described with a laugh, as a "striking" animal companion. Though the other snakes in their home were cool, only Flip liked to crawl in her hair and nestle there while she walked around, did dishes, watched a movie or read. With his instinctive ability to perceive vibrations, he also shared her love of music. He did, however, have his preferences. Put on a Curtis Mayfield CD, with its funky, heavy bass beat, and Flip would pop his head out of her hair to groove with her. Put on Jane's Addiction, music ruled by high-pitched vocals and offbeat guitar lines, and he'd retreat under her hair every time.

Tuning in on the snake proved to be more demanding for Sharon than with Killer and Fink. Though Flip was not refusing to communicate, she found herself immersed in a misty, dreamlike state of consciousness that went beyond the recognizable lethargy of hibernation. Producing no distinct word or thought transfers, the visual flow she perceived was cosmic and impersonal.

Accompanied by gauzy scenes of the snake being safely confined within a tight place, Flip indicated that he was wedged in a small opening in a corner; he wasn't sure where, as it was all unfamiliar to him.

Aware that snakes often don't understand boundaries, Ariel asked Sharon if the corner was in the couple's house, or if Flip had wandered even further away. If he had, that bothered her; for she was concerned that he might get injured or eaten.

The animal communicator replied that he felt not far away and that *wander* was a good verb to use. For she sensed Flip was at heart an adventurer. He was also a thinker. Cocooned now in the tight space surrounded by walls, he was coiled in self-reflection.

Communicating that that was precisely what he was doing, Flip informed the animal intuitive that he was trying to figure out where he was headed after his hibernation period. He loved Ariel very much, and, yes, he missed crawling in her hair and helping her do things, but he didn't miss his terrarium.

Ariel commented that she wasn't surprised to hear that, as her boy wasn't like most snakes, that is, happy to get out for awhile, but eager to be back home to hide away. Also, a few weeks before he left, she'd noticed that he seemed to be figuring out how to open his chopsticks box, sliding the cage top with his nose.

Flip projected on Sharon's mind screen a picture of his pushing the top open just enough to squeeze through and be free. Freedom was as important to him as food and warmth, Sharon observed. A free spirit, Flip was one who could not be content being confined.

Ariel would understand that, the snake communicated to the animal intuitive, for he was simply a mirror of her independent spirit, her love of the unexplored. Sometimes, though, his human companion, with her demanding financial work, didn't allow that joyful energy to break out. Flip said his foray into the unknown was to remind her to occasionally abscond from routine to experience the newness of life.

As her mirror, his adventurous exit also reflected another positive quality that Ariel must employ at this moment and in the future: trust. She must remember to not only trust the Universe that all things were going to work out fine, but also to trust herself, her own guidance.

Ending his communication with Sharon, Flip sent one last scene to the animal intuitive to give to his cherished human companion. Walking down a path, with Flip's silky body wrapped around her, Ariel stops to let him slide onto the ground to continue his journey. Lovingly, he holds on for a moment longer, then moves boldly forward. She wishes him well no matter what his decision, but if he does decide to return home, she promises him that things will be different.

As she finished with Flip's vision story, Sharon explained how Ariel could fulfill Flip's message. She was to mentally portray to the snake that when he returned home, he wouldn't be put in a snake house and that he could be free to head out again on a search-and-experience mission any time. Ariel heartily agreed.

With Kyle on the extension phone, he joined Ariel to ask Sharon about Saratoga. Slipping into the King snake's field of energy, Sharon noted that on a communication level, it was difficult recognizing her as a snake. In fact, she told the couple, if she didn't already know she was merging into a snake's energy field, she would have thought Saratoga was a self-assured dog or a cat. Not only was her ease in being in a human-oriented environment apparent, but also her communication skills spoke volumes. Literally. Unlike the other three snakes, she communicated directly with words, speaking in a clear, androgynous voice that Sharon could easily hear.

In fact, the intelligent reptile reported to the animal communicator that she liked words. Picking up the emotional vibrations of thought or dialogue was an entertaining exercise. She loved to be around Ariel and Kyle when they talked to one another, watched a movie on TV or read, whether silently or out loud to her.

Describing her life as a harmonious one, she said that she also enjoyed, as opposed to most of those of her species, activity around her. When the house was abuzz with people visiting her human partners, she wanted to be involved. The more she was handled, the more she felt included. Her gregarious nature was another factor in her role as Kyle and Ariel's sacred companion. For Kyle, her open and joyful attitude toward people in a social situation was a mirror that reflected the art of learning to be more trusting and less anxious around others. For Ariel, who was in her element when hosting others in her home, it was an affirmation of her powerful, compassionate female self.

At this point, Sharon asked the young couple if they had any questions for Saratoga. Replying that they didn't, for "their girl" Saratoga's personal report had, not unexpectedly, already supplied them with plenty of answers and plenty of things to think about.

Saratoga said she had one other thing to say. She spoke for not only herself but for Fink, Flip and Killer as well. Not only was she looking forward to the condominiums Kyle was working hard on, but also she was looking forward to continuing to serve as a dedicated animal companion for him and Ariel for as long as needed.

As the reading closed down, Sharon ended the session by complimenting the two on how well they cared for their animal companions. However, she told them, their attention and love for their beloved companions had a payoff of its own. As dynamic energy beings, snakes exude an incredible life force, she explained, that not only binds to those whom they feel attachment, but their dynamic energy also serves as a physical conduit to staying connected to the wild, something that was critical for both Kyle and Ariel.

Concluding, Sharon suggested that the couple remember what their animal companions had reflected to them and that they stay open to all possibilities, as they continued to treasure this special friendship they had with Saratoga, Killer, Flip and Fink.

Nearly a year later, the animal intuitive received an email from Kyle and Ariel about their snake family. Saratoga and Killer were fine; Flip had not returned, but Fink had been found during some recent plumbing work in their bathroom. Discovered in a reopened wall space, the thin and dehydrated snake had apparently crawled through an access hole during repair work last fall and had been sealed up for almost nine months. Ariel wrote that as she held the flashlight, Kyle had retrieved his frail buddy from the darkened gap. Glad to be back in their arms, Fink had only wanted to be under Kyle's collar. Their animal companion was pretty much back to normal in demeanor, weight and body coloring, except he now had freckles sprinkled over his body. Kyle, of course, was thrilled Fink had survived and had been holding on all that time for him. Fink had taught him a lot about faith, trust and not being afraid of the unfamiliar.

Ariel still wished her boy Flip would reappear, but she wasn't even sure if he was still alive. By striking out on his own, he had reflected her own joy for life and adventure, and reminded her to cherish it no matter what the consequences.

Saratoga, a Goin's King snake.

Killer, a Honduran Milk snake.

Fink, a Thayer's King snake.

Thanking Sharon again for her help, Ariel signed off by noting that with Fink back home with Saratoga and Killer, she and Kyle were once again "en-(w)rap-tured" by their animal companions.

Later, as the animal communicator updated their file, Sharon realized that the story of Kyle and Ariel's relationship with their serpents, animal companions most people couldn't appreciate, was not only singular, it was inspirational. It resonated perfectly with a compelling sentence from *The Black Stallion*, a story she'd favored as a child: "The friendship between the boy and the stallion was something too much for them to understand."

14

KEEPING THE FAITH

Master said God had given men reason, by
which they could find out things for themselves,
but He had given animals knowledge which
did not depend on reason, and which was
more prompt and perfect in its way

Black Beauty, Anna Sewell

ushing the cleansing solution across the kitchen floor with the sponge mop, Catherine hoped the rhythm would shake her out of the monotony of another day. Not that she minded her work. Cleaning houses for others was honorable work, one that she was paid well for. Knowing that she was readying their homes for another week of uncluttered and spotless living gave her pleasure. Usually.

Today, however, she felt anxious, unsettled. Maybe because today marked the three-month anniversary of Kippie's passing. She still missed the dwarf rabbit, the first lagomorph (new word for her then) she'd ever been around. With this special rabbit's friendship, Catherine had overcome a difficult time in her life. But now, with her animal companion no longer around, she felt less anchored and more alone than she thought possible.

And, yet, there was something else that gnawed at her beyond her heartache. Something she couldn't quite define.

Swabbing the last section of the tile floor, she returned to her work. But her thoughts kept returning to Kippie. It was as if her old pal were there with her, urging her to have faith in her inner guidance system that was detecting something askew.

Following that lead, she walked into the den and, with her forehead against the windowpane, she scoured the outside area. Though nothing nabbed her eye, she felt a presence. An energy so faint, it reminded her of a smoke detector crippled by a fading battery, emitting its last strident, mournful beeps.

Suddenly the word *rabbits* leaped across her mind's eye. Confused, she found herself insisting aloud that there were no rabbits out there. She'd worked here for over six years and had never seen any. Then she remembered that her client had mentioned something about having rabbits before. But that was a few years back.

Opening the back door, she walked outside and quickly scanned the place for any clues that would explain the surreal message, as well as her uneasiness. But nothing she saw—lawn furniture, a grill, flower containers, a gardening table, old, rejected cages—seemed amiss.

Then her eyes returned to the cages tucked away in a far corner. Squinting her eyes to telescope her vision, she saw an indiscriminate lump huddling in one of the shabby coops. Nearing the small, filthy metal cages, she saw that the lump was a rabbit. Barely breathing, the sore-covered creature was without food and water. And she looked as if she had been that way for a while.

Unlatching the cage, she slowly placed her hand on the gray bunny, but the rabbit did not move. She was either catatonic or dead. Yet the woman felt a sliver of warmness coming from the fur. Though relieved that she was alive, Catherine noticed that she was on her last leg, if she even had working legs. She still hadn't moved.

Running back to the house to call her employer, the woman whom she would have never suspected of such neglect, Catherine decided she was going to ask to take the animal home tonight, if the poor animal could survive till then.

On the phone, she listened as the lady of the house offhandedly explained that the rabbits had been an Easter present and they had always lived out there. When a taken-aback Catherine asked why she said, "they," the woman replied that there had been three, but with one of them dying a few months ago, there were now only two left.

With an effort to keep her voice from quivering as her heart was doing, Catherine inquired how long they had been there. About eight years, she was told, because her daughter got them when she was in grade school and she was now a sophomore in college.

Taking a deep breath, Catherine asked if she might have them, as she was a big fan of rabbits. The woman said she'd have to check with her daughter and would let Catherine know.

Quickly Catherine returned to the yard with some water for the gray rabbit. Searching the shed, she found some old rabbit food and offered a huge helping to the malnourished bunny.

She then focused on finding the other rabbit. Noticing that one of the top cages had a shingle overhead, one on the far back corner and another on the right side forming a dark corner, she leaned forward for a closer look. Crouched there was a trembling, chocolate Dutch rabbit with broken teeth and a body almost as thin as her gray neighbor's.

Opening her cage, she slowly moved toward the animal, speaking lovingly to her. With gentle strokes, she petted her head. The rabbit appeared bewildered by Catherine's touch. And when Catherine gave her food and water, she seemed only more so, as if she'd forgotten the familiar routine of eating and drinking.

Not knowing how long it would be before she got the word from her employer, she placed some old, soft cleaning cloths she'd retrieved from her car in their cages. They would provide warmth and ease the pain that the cold wire floors undoubtedly inflicted on the rabbits' feet pads. Scabs evidenced that.

Leaving them was hard, but the wait was the hardest. Four days would pass before her employer would call. During those 96 hours, Catherine felt like a kid waiting for Christmas to come. From antici-pating the joy the event would bring to thinking maybe it would never come, she felt tossed around like clothes in a scorching dryer.

But she had to believe that the bunnies would not only survive, but also that they would soon be with her. However, having faith had never been easy for her. From people to situations, she had often seen the flip side of faith: disappointment and distrust. A sensitive being, she knew that both could extract deep pain too much to endure.

Yet, here were two bare-boned creatures showing her that all things can be endured if you keep your heart full of hope. And when her client phoned with the okay, Catherine found herself tiptoeing toward believing again in the goodness of life, as surely as she raced back to the rabbits.

At the bunnies' dilapidated, fecal-littered cages, though, her new resolve wavered for a moment. Shaking her head at the physical state of these neglected creatures who had lived in all kinds of weather (the summer high could easily go to 110 degrees; the winter low to 25 degrees), Catherine felt her stomach lurch at the sheer nastiness of their shoe box–size homes. Even if she weren't a woman who took pride in her cleaning abilities, she'd still be nauseated at the conditions these two imprisoned animals were forced to endure. Yet, she knew her employers were not intentionally uncaring people, and she would never judge their actions or, rather, inactions.

Announcing to the animals that there was no way she was going to transport those disgusting cages to her house, she removed her fleece. Gently wrapping the soft jacket around the featherweight rabbits— neither one could be over three pounds—she secured them in her arms, carried them to her car and drove them home.

Using eyedroppers, Catherine gave the bunnies water, food and medication. Both were beginning to respond to the TLC, though Catherine knew they were still unsure about being handled. As it had obviously been a long time since they'd been touched, and being creatures of prey genetically programmed to flee, she wouldn't have been surprised to witness an attempt to hide under the sofa.

But that wasn't an option for Beatrice, the name Catherine had conferred on the tiny gray female. Her back legs were severely crippled. And although the other female, dubbed Snickers, could use her legs, she was still so weak and confused, the frail rabbit made no efforts to do so.

Besides those concerns, Catherine knew the rest of them needed mending as well, but she had a possible panacea for that. She'd already acquired an appointment with an animal intuitive who had helped her with Kippie. With her communication skills and her own flower essences, Sharon Callahan just might be the mediator her new animal companions needed.

Merging with Beatrice and Snickers because both, having survived together, wanted to tell their stories together, the animal intuitive communicated with them by way of feeling images. Sharon explained to Catherine that this method was not uncommon for abused animals. With their feelings, the most basic component of all beings, as the brush, and her mind as the canvas, the two were free to paint their story pictures.

Though they had been cared for reasonably well in the beginning by the young girl, they expressed to Sharon, the last six years had been rough. Delegated to the back corner of the yard in cages that didn't provide adequate shelter, the two rabbits—once there were three, but the third died from dehydration—had spent their time encouraging one another to survive another day. Watering and feedings were sporadic, subject to their human caretakers' remembering they were there. Malnutrition and the tightly confined space of her cage had deformed Bea's body and crippled her back legs. Snickers, blessed with a sturdier constitution and a somewhat larger cage by inches, had always been the stronger of the two, though it had been a long time since she could be labeled strong.

But those were the physical manifestations of the neglect. The deepest suffering came from the absence of love and touch. It had been years since they had been held. Being touched by a caring human hand was not only a forgotten experience, but in separate cages, they couldn't even huddle together.

Yet, Beatrice and Snickers conveyed to Sharon, they could do one thing. They could help each other to keep the faith. Encouraging each other, they held fast to the belief that one day life would be more than capricious nourishment in a small, wire cage, where movement was restricted and their feces were constant cell mates.

When Catherine expressed her dismay at their having to live in the bleak enclosure, the rabbits told Sharon that cages weren't found only in their world. Didn't humans often put themselves in rigid, uncaring belief cages? Sadly, they confined themselves by not believing in themselves enough to listen and trust their inner guidance system, their heart. Or they caged themselves by believing they were so omniscient about life, they not only had it all figured out, but they also were the only beings on earth who had real intelligence, feelings, thoughts and interests. "Both of those cages," Snickers and Bea pointed out to the animal intuitive, "suffocate love and respect for all life, as well as one's self."

Continuing their story, the animal companions explained how they came to escape their cages. Although they were focused on staying alive, nevertheless, the day before Catherine found them, Beatrice began to fade. Snickers, feeling her friend's near departure, pushed hard against her own cage toward Beatrice, but it was futile, she described in the feeling images she was sending to Sharon.

Beatrice communicated that at this juncture, she thought she was nearing her time to leave. With no reserves left, she was thirsty, hungry and feverish. When she saw a blue-light presence, she thought it had come to escort her. But the loving essence said if the rabbit could hold on for just a while longer, an angel would come to help her and Snickers. The angel would be in the form of a human being who would faithfully and tenderly care for them. In turn, she and Snickers, as her animal companions, would help the woman.

Sharon asked Catherine if she were familiar with animal companion mirroring. Catherine answered that she wasn't sure. Explaining it as a form of service to their human partners, Sharon said animals often reflect to us what we need to know about ourselves to grow in spirit and keep our lives in balance. For Catherine, lack of faith had not only made her fearful of life, but it also had kept her isolated. Beatrice and Snickers mirrored, through their holding on against great odds, a wonderful, tangible example of faith in action. Over the next few months, they would help their human companion with another issue, for their love was unconditionally faithful.

To help all three during this time of adjustment, the animal communicator suggested to Catherine that they take advantage of nature's flower power. Two flower essences that had helped her clients in the past for such emotional wear-and-tear were Baby Blue Eyes, which encouraged one to move forward with faith, trust and hope despite past harm, and Forget-me-not, a good first-aid remedy that accented life's positive aspects.

As the session concluded, Catherine promised the rabbits they'd never suffer again. And over the next six months, Beatrice and Snickers emerged into the world of abundance. Treats such as dandelions, parsley, apples, raisins and bananas made eating a gourmet event for the emaciated rabbits who before had only known dried, stale food occasionally dropped into their cage.

Fresh greens were indeed an exotic meal, but fresh green grass under their paws was also a sheer delight. Unlike Peter Rabbit, they had never experienced the vegetables of Mr. Macgregor's garden. In fact, they had never known the outside as a truly hospitable place.

But now, embraced by the rich aroma and feel of grass, and Catherine beside them, the outside was no longer a place for the bunnies to survive in, it was a place to enjoy the unimpeded exhilaration of bunny hopping. Though Bea's back legs would never return to normal, she managed to join Snickers in this true lagomorph movement.

Shelter was inside their human companion's home. Each had a roomy hutch with a ramp. When Catherine was out of the house, they stayed in their cottage, as Catherine proudly called it, and rooted in the sweet-smelling hay. When she was home, they were where she was.

But life's new abundance was most pronounced in the love they received and expressed. Making their unique noises and bebopping around—with her limp legs, Bea rolled—the rabbits joined Catherine in singing and dancing. Other times, they sat beside, or on, Catherine and listened to *Angel Music*, their favorite harp CD. No matter what the activity, Snickers and Bea reflected to Catherine the power of nurturing both the physical and the spiritual bodies

At times, their mirroring would take Catherine back to two years ago when she had taken a detour on her career path. Although she cleaned homes for her basic income, she was also a neophyte spiritual counselor. Her natural ability to help many through spiritual awakenings as well as crises did not go unnoticed. As she became more and more busy, she found herself so immersed in others' cares that she began to feel as if she were drowning, too. Doubt set in, and she left the field.

But she knew her heart never left. Without faith in herself, however, she couldn't return. Except for Kippie, she sought solace in solitude. Cleaning houses while her clients were at work afforded that. When Kippie passed, she was even more alone, that is, until two rabbits hopped unexpectedly into the picture.

When Catherine called Sharon several months later with an update on Snicks and Bea (funny, she thought, how familiarity breeds truncated nicknames), she reported that both were doing well. Maybe even too well, she laughed, as they were both getting a little plump in their old age. Cutting back on treats could be a good option for her animal companions' health.

Now using sharper mental images, as well as thoughts, the rabbits communicated to Sharon that they'd rather not have their present diet tampered with, thank you very much. Each blamed the other for over eating and, like healthy, happy "siblings," teased the other. Snicks said Bea was nice, but an airhead; Bea retorted that Snicks was beautiful, but not very smart.

Laughing, Sharon said one of the best things in communicating with animals was seeing their distinct personalities unfold. Animals, she said to Catherine, were no different from humans: just as they had souls, thoughts, feelings and jobs, they had personalities.

Catherine said she knew the girls had all those things, especially jobs. For she had to admit they were doing their mirroring jobs just fine. With their lessons in faith, as well as their showing her that she could nurture without losing herself, she had begun to work as a spiritual counselor again. Not that she didn't still have some leaps and bounds to make in her own growth, but what better animal companions to have around to show her how to do that than rabbits?

Two years later, Sharon received an e-mail from Catherine. Her beloved Snicks and Bea had passed away, only a few days apart. She still missed them. But knowing that she had given them the best while they were with her and that they were being watched over as they took their next journey, she was able to send them light and let them go. Her counseling work was continuing to blossom, and she knew she could only thank them for their love and faithfulness that went beyond reason.

As Sharon printed the e-mail and placed it in Catherine's file, the animal intuitive was reminded of a quote from *Black Beauty*. Its wisdom seemed to aptly depict the messages Snicks and Bea had given to us all: "Master said God had given men reason, by which they could find out things for themselves, but He had given animals knowledge which did not depend on reason, and which was more prompt and perfect in its way."

Bea and Snickers.

15

LIVING IN THE HERE AND NOW

Like nearly all dogs, as well as practically all children that have not been blocked in their natural growing and expanding, Strongheart was a master of the art of living fully and completely in the here and now of things.

Kinship with All Life, J. Alan Boone

Sunshine, a **Shiba** Inu dog in Paris, France, was a conundrum to his human companion. The yellow canine's unexplained behaviors were not only a puzzle for Jeanne Bidot but also for the three trainers she'd gone through trying to nose Sunshine onto a trail of reliable and obedient conduct.

An aggressive barker, he was just as avid in his attempts to harass and race after other dogs, especially females, though once he was with other dogs, he acted like a social misfit, awkward and unfriendly. Walks in the park also instigated another obsession. Gobbling down any food leftovers he came across, the already well-fed dog was always adamantly on the lookout for scraps.

In the house, Sunshine fidgeted, especially at night. Though the veterinarian had given him a clean bill of health, he exhibited other baffling actions that the vet could not determine a physical reason for, including drinking *beaucoup* amounts of water and either holding it in or peeing erratically on the floor.

Jeanne had hoped that having an animal companion would add a positive note to her life; however, now she found that, though she knew she and Sunshine seemed to have a deep connection, the dog's actions and moods were having the opposite effect. With her own life in the doghouse in many ways (her stressful job, her social life in disarray and her weight a constant battle), she needed some answers.

In her quest for help to better understand Sunshine, she began researching online, at the library and at the bookstore, for information about animals and their behaviors. In the "Resources" section at the back of one animal book, she found Sharon's business listing.

Because of time constraints, Sharon rarely took nonreferred requests for consultations, but even in English Jeanne's request conveyed such an earnest desire to have Sharon communicate with her dog that she felt guided to agree to a reading.

Jeanne said she called the animal intuitive because she wanted to be close to her dog. But how could that be when he didn't even obey her? She also wanted to figure out how to handle Sunshine, to understand why he was acting the way he did. She hoped Sharon could decode his inexplicable mannerisms that no amount of training could alter.

Fusing with Sunshine, Sharon was flooded with a plethora of visual images. And although most animals spoke with feelings and some pictures, his photo album was more like an action film. His emotional language was just as impressive. Exuding a proud independence, along with a great affection for his human companion, his energy was powerful and confident. Immediately, he informed Sharon that Jeanne need not try to have a spiritual connection to him, for as her sacred companion, he was already tied to her. Had she not dreamed about a yellow dog before she bought him?

Sunshine relayed that he was neither ill nor distressed, he was simply mirroring his beloved human companion's own behaviors. He was also bringing her the important message of living life and addressing life's issues, not with regret for the past, nor with worry for the future, but in the beauty of the here and now.

With pictures of a restless canine sent to Sharon, he said he fidgeted at night because, with Jeanne's anxiety about her career and future, she did. Transmitting feelings of confusion, he communicated that he didn't understand why she went to work at a place she didn't like. As Sharon noted this, Jeanne confirmed that she was unhappy with her professional life. Although the American corporation she worked for offered security, the demands of the high-powered job, long hours and constant stress often negated any satisfaction in her career. More than once, she'd thought of leaving, but that too brought its own stress, including fitful sleep during the night. During those times, she'd often awake thinking that Sunshine's pacing or jumping on and off the bed had roused her.

As Sunshine showed Sharon scenes of his wolfing down food scraps on their walks in the park, he pointed out that he turned his nose up at nourishing leftovers and only ate the fast food, the greasy fries and burgers. His copious snacking had nothing to do with hunger, for she fed him well, but it did have much to do with Jeanne. His dietary habits reflected hers. When she stopped downing lots of unhealthy food, so would he. Plus, that kind of food, especially when compared to the nutritious food she gave him at home, did tend to make him more jumpy than normal. Though, he confessed, he did like the taste of it.

When Sharon shared that information with Jeanne, they both laughed, as the animal empath added that animals, like humans, have their own personalities. Some are serious, while some have a distinct sense of humor. Sunshine was of the latter.

Confessing that she often turned to fast food for quick meals and sweets for comfort, Jeanne said she knew it wasn't healthy for her. And though she was obdurate about making sure Sunshine had the best dog food available, she knew she was not as devoted to her own health care. That was something she was always going to work on tomorrow, she admitted, and somehow it never became the here and now.

Sunshine then offered images of his drinking large amounts of water from his bowl. His large consumption of water wasn't because he was thirsty, and its erratic release wasn't because he had a physical problem. It was his eye-catching way of showing her she needed to drink more of the cleansing liquid herself. As her animal companion, so linked to her, he was mirroring that the best way he knew how.

But Sunshine indicated to Sharon that most of his acting-out behaviors were reflections of Jeanne's fear of trusting and living life in the moment. Her fear of getting close to people socially or intimately was reflected to her in Sunshine's inappropriate barking. Unabated barking is one way a dog holds others at a distance. His inability to be comfortable around other dogs or people was a reflection of Jeanne's distrust. As for working with a dog trainer, well, he pointed out, he wasn't going to change his habits until she cared enough about herself to change hers, for he was bonded to her in heart, was a loyal companion and really wanted to be a good boy.

Once again, Jeanne agreed that Sunshine was right on target about her fears, though it was sometimes hard to acknowledge. She'd tell herself that because she worked long hours at the office, she didn't have time for a social life. Or because she wasn't happy with her physical appearance, she was not ready for a romantic liaison. And there was the past littered with old relationship disappointments. Yet she knew that keeping herself aloof from others had its own price.

To help Sunshine physically and emotionally, Sharon asked Jeanne to consider having the canine neutered. But the most effectual step toward assisting Sunshine to balance his behaviors and feelings was for his human companion to have an honest look at hers and set herself on an even keel. Jeanne might also consider a calming flower essence formula for Sunshine. The formula included Water Hemlock for promoting a calm and steady inner and outer presence—it was especially good for high-strung sensitive animals in training—and Shasta Daisy, useful for introducing a new behavior.

The last time Sharon heard from Jeanne, Sunshine was the epitome of his name. Full of spirited joy, Sunshine was more in control of himself and pleased to be mirroring a woman who had also taken control of herself. Jeanne was making a career move and nourishing her body with a balanced diet. Though both had more adjusting and growing to do, Sunshine and Jeanne communicated that each was committed. Sunshine added he was pleased to be performing this service, for that was what spiritual companions did: they served one another, as they lived in the here and now.

As Sharon completed her notes on Sunshine, she thought about the message that this frisky dog from France brought to his human companion and to her. A message that often needs repeating because people, including herself, tend to forget is that, though nostalgia and planning have their place in our lives, all anyone ever really has is the moment. And to live life to the fullest is to be not only aware of the now, but to enjoy that moment, just as J. Alan Boone had written about through the dog Strongheart in his book *Kinship with All Life*: "Like nearly all dogs, as well as practically all children that have not been blocked in their natural growing and expanding, Strongheart was a master of the art of living fully and completely in the here and now of things."

Sunshine, the Shiba Inu.

16

AGING WITH GRACE

*He even began to lose his shape, and he scarcely
looked like a rabbit anymore, except to the Boy.
To him he was always beautiful and that was
all that the little Rabbit cared about.*

The Velveteen Rabbit, Margery Williams Bianco

Through the camera's viewfinder, she inspected the image: a white and tan Brittany-Lab mix posed gracefully with freshly cut purple irises by his side. As she clicked the photograph from various angles, Laney's thoughts rewound to the past for a moment. For there was a time when she would have shot the scene differently here in her studio. Ben, ever the dashing poser, would have been holding the bouquet in his teeth. And after that portrait, he would have been ready for more, eager to sit for any scene and don any accessories Laney had for him. He'd even served as ring bearer at her wedding 12 years ago. And though the marriage hadn't lasted, Ben's commitment to *putting on the dog* for Laney's shots had.

But no more. Now nearly 20 years old the canine, who had sat for scores of studio shots and hundreds of outside candid shots, had seen the last of youthful days where energy and physical beauty came as easily as retrieving a spinning Frisbee.

Laney remembered the first time she saw Ben. Recuperating from being hit by a car, he was in a roomy, post-surgery cage at the animal clinic where she regularly took her birds and rabbit for care. Known to the staff as someone who took good care of her animal companions, Laney had received a call from her vet one cold Idaho afternoon. He asked her if she'd be willing to adopt a badly injured dog who he had found along the roadside that icy morning. The dog had been hit by a car and would need lots of special attention. Held together by pins, his leg had been crushed and, coupled with other injuries, he wouldn't be able to walk for several months. Plus, the veterinarian cautioned Laney, the dog would need more surgeries ahead, and the future would never be a sure thing.

When she walked up to Ben in his enclosure a day later and their eyes exchanged that first take, Laney knew there was something there, something indefinable, a deep spiritual connection that electrified her and yet soothed her. For the next two weeks, she visited him regularly. Sitting in his enclosure with him, she stroked the dog, talking to him about her home, the place he would soon call home.

She began taking pictures of him, capturing the canine's energy not only with her eyes' reliable acuity, which had gained her recognition in her profession, but also with her third eye, that singular perception that came from beyond the mundane. A shot of Ben peering through the bars of his pen with a crooked smile was page one of a scrapbook that would feature Ben's life over a span of many albums.

When Laney brought her new animal companion home, she continued taking Ben's images, but her biggest priority was caring for him. With the pins in his left rear limb, Ben was unable to stand and support his weight. Walking outside to use the toilet was impossible. To assist him, Laney would place a towel under his belly in front of his hind legs. Lifting the towel raised his rear legs, allowing him to maneuver forward on his front ones as she walked him from behind. Once outside, she'd whipped the towel out as he hunkered down to do his business. That done, Laney would secure the towel back under his legs and wheelbarrow him back inside, not knowing then that Ben and she would return to the wheelbarrow theme in a different and powerful way one day. The pins in his leg also deterred him from resting well and at times she'd massage the rest of his body, hoping to get Ben to focus on the gentle rubbing instead of the intense pain he was experiencing.

With the injury site draining, much attention was also needed to keep the area clean and protected. But Ben never whined, complained or tried to bite, even during the numerous exams, treatments, surgeries and wee-hours-of-the-night trips to the emergency room, required in the months that followed his settling in at her place. And Laney, with her husband Daryl's support and their new animal companion's stoicism, also stayed on task.

In a year's time, Ben's leg healed, and though he would always walk with a limp, he became a functional part of the family. He even learned to accept Bonsai the rabbit as a buddy, not prey to chase. During those years, he and Laney became the best of buds themselves. In their youthful prime, he was now 8 and she was 30, they traveled everywhere together in her little truck with the top open. From work assignments to impulsive trips to parks and the canyons, the two cruised the roads with glee.

It was then, long before it became fashionable via calendars and greeting cards, that Ben began wearing sunglasses. Placing the shades on his face to keep the debris out while riding down the road in the truck, Laney decided the dark glasses actually made her animal companion look as cool as any debonair gentleman. Ben must have agreed, for he didn't try then, nor would he ever try, to remove them. Sitting with his paw on the car's armrest and wearing his sunglasses, he was the epitome of cool, "a regular James Bond," Laney told him laughingly.

But sometimes Ben could carry his mission of being a close working and play partner too far. Stopping at a department store at a nearby mall one hot summer's day, Laney ran into the store to pick up some linens, leaving Ben to wait in the open-top automobile. As she sorted through the items on the shelf, she heard a commotion in the store, a commotion that was racing closer and closer to her. Looking down the aisle, she saw a sunglasses-clad Ben speeding toward her, followed by three store employees and several customers, all shouting "stop that dog!" Obviously, she and her traveling partner were asked to leave immediately. How her animal companion managed to enter the store so easily, she was never to know for sure. But she figured he'd learned how to get in by watching, from his observation post in the truck, customers use the automatic entry door. And when he tried it himself, decked out in his chic sunglasses, she guessed he appeared to fit right in.

A few days after that event, he even managed to find her inside a crowded grocery store. After that, she had to give Ben a good talking-to. Though it was hard to lecture him with a straight face, as he would look at her as if to question why he, a dog, couldn't go shopping, too.

At the dog park, however, Ben never faced such separatists' rules. Free to enjoy the surroundings, he knew the only ones chasing him would be his fun-seeking canine pals. To capture them in their play, Laney began shooting images of them from their perspective. Photographing dogs was certainly nothing new for her. Besides taking copious pictures of Ben, she'd spent several years as a photographer for dog shows around the country and often did portraits locally of people and their animal companions. But catching these enthusiastic creatures in everyday candid moments at their height level was a novel concept for her. And Ben, with his joy for being with her, his friends and the birds he'd chase (and never seem to actually want to capture), rewarded her with some wonderful images. During those days, she also experimented with various modalities, including infrared and digital photography.

Tonight, putting away her digital camera, the tripod, the lights and sitting down in front of her laptop to view the stills she'd just shot, Laney found herself looking back at some of the earlier pics she'd taken of Ben. Though he'd come to live with her when he was a seven-year-old adult, even then, with his goofy grin, he seemed so much younger. But so did she. Moving closer to the computer screen, she stared at one of her favorite pictures: With Ben on her tummy, she was lying down on her back, the two of them facing the camera in obvious bliss.

Look at my eyes, she thought. They're not puffy and certainly not creased. They're so compact, lighter, unmarked by time. She grabbed a mirror that clients used for last minute touch-ups and peered at the face before her. She was 42 and not the tomboy of her early years, so full of zest and zoom on her skateboard; she was not the photographer travel-ing the country in a van where days and nights often merged, and she was not the young bride at the beach with her groom and canine ring bearer. In those days, she never considered that her no-need-for-makeup face would change. Though she could look at her family and see that hooded eyes often came with age, it was never a concern for her. She was too busy dancing with life.

Returning to her laptop, she clicked through the visual memories on disc, as she reached over to Ben sitting on her desk where she had placed him after the shoot. Laney rubbed his head. He sighed, presented his familiar grin and slowly opened his eyes when he felt her familiar touch. Once clear and bright, they were now cloudy. The vet had told her, when she'd taken Ben in for a recent checkup four months ago, that her sweet canine buddy could only see shadowy, opaque figures in various shades of dark and light. When she asked Dr. Laura about Ben's changing body—arthritis had set in and walking was now out of the question—and if there was anything she could do for her beloved animal companion during this stage of his life, the vet had given her many useful tips. But the veterinarian couldn't answer some of Laney's questions about Ben. Instead, she had suggested Laney call someone who probably could: an animal intuitive in the mountains of northern California whose work she respected. Sharon Callahan had helped several of her patients in the past, and Dr. Laura said she suspected the animal communicator could help Laney, too.

Laney called that night for an appointment, but was disappointed to learn Sharon's first opening wasn't for another four months. But Laney, feeling comfortable already with the intuitive, made an appointment. Before she hung up, Sharon had asked if Laney had a photo of Ben that she could send her. Laughing, Laney responded that she just might have a few!

On the phone with Sharon that night as scheduled, Laney began by asking the animal communicator what she could do to help Ben. Merging with the dog, Sharon shared with Laney that Ben communicated with pictures—they came easily to him as he was around photography and images so much he said—and with word feelings, that is, she explained, she could understand what he was saying via empathically feeling what he was feeling. Ben, she noted to Laney, liked to talk. He thought he was a good communicator and a good mirror, if Laney would be willing to look in it.

Pointing out that mirroring was an important task that animal companions take on in their relationship with their human friends, Sharon said Ben was handling his role with pride. But first, before he would communicate about his mirroring work, he wanted Laney to know that he loved her dearly, for they were old, old friends. And as a close buddy, he wanted her to know that he wished she'd remember something that she seemed to forget at times: who she is. A competent, kind human being who has no need to worry about getting things right all the time or being good enough. As if only being perfect made one okay, or acceptable. If he'd listened to that kind of logic, he communicated to Sharon, he'd have been a goner a long time ago. Laney, he continued, must understand that we are not the sum of our work, our plans, our tangible products, but our hearts. And Laney had a big one.

He also wanted her to know that he appreciated all she had done in her caring for him, from the day she first brought her compassion to the animal clinic to be with him, to her taking him with her on all her outings, to her tending to him now, especially. Sharon hesitated for a moment, then told Laney she was receiving a picture of a wheelbarrow and asked if she wished to talk about the wheelbarrow.

Explaining that the wheelbarrow was how she and her partner Theo now took Ben on his walk up to the school yard where he had once played, Laney said that Ben and his blanket-wrapped wheelbarrow were a familiar sight in the neighborhood. Apparently it was quite the attraction, as people would stop and ask about Ben and his story. They always seemed to be surprised that he was as old as he was, and they'd inevitably say how really good he looked.

Interrupting, Ben communicated that he found it odd that human beings were so focused on not only one's past but also on how old one was. It seemed to him that only today mattered, as that was all you really had within your reach anyway. And as for the age concern, that was a scent he couldn't follow. Surely, growing older was a natural part of life. The key, he figured, was not trying to avoid aging, but learning to age with grace. That was what, he told the animal communicator, he was trying to reflect to Laney, for lately he'd noticed that his human companion had been paying more attention to her age. Was Laney aware of this?

Responding that she guessed she was, though, Laney confessed, she'd never realized she was giving it much thought, especially since her mane was still rich and thick, her figure slim and her energy level still high. She actually believed she looked good for her age, but she had noticed some changes. She was developing little fatty-tissue deposits on the top of her arms, like her uncle had. Also, now when her skin changed color and became more puffy with stress, it took longer for it to return to normal, plus her eyes were beginning to droop a tad. She used to say when she was at an age when filling out her birth date on a form didn't give her any second thoughts that she'd just have surgery when she got older. It was hard to think she might be there, yet lately when she was around the 20-something women at work, the thought slipped in the back door. For she had noticed that this new feeling of being aware of her age was about more than possessing unscathed looks, it was also about how society responds to you. Explaining that she had observed people acting differently, more positively, toward a younger face, Laney said she had also noticed that it just seemed things—life— came more easily for those not heading toward middle age.

Ben communicated the image of a mirror to Sharon noting that, as Laney's mirror, he had been reflecting a way for her to approach aging with panache. Here he was in a fragile body, nearly blind, unable to walk, and yet he didn't mind at all, for he knew he beamed with a spirited glow: a beauty that sparkled beyond the thinning hair, the sagging skin and the ungainly shape of the body. People were drawn to him in the wheelbarrow not because he was a dog in a wheelbarrow, but because he was dog who didn't *mind* being in a wheelbarrow. He was happy and proud of his life and the body that had carried him through it. Using this template, Ben hoped, would help Laney center herself as she moved further along in her journey. It was imperative that she see the changes in her body as evidence that she resides in a place in the Universe where time may indeed be a great chiseler of the physical body, but can also be a great teacher for the spiritual body. For wisdom, he added, was something youth could not buy.

Concluding the session, Sharon said that Ben had left her with one bright image: a skateboard. He said Laney would know what she was to do with that. On the other end of the phone, Laney, wiping her eyes, caught her breath. She told the animal intuitive that since she was seven she'd been riding skateboards. Longboards, shortboards, she was versatile with them all, doing 360s, going up on the front end of a long board and tipping it so that the back wheels were up. She knew a myriad of tricks. But lately, when she'd go up to the schoolyard near her and see the kids with their menu of tricks spawned from their generation, she found herself thinking if she'd do that, she'd fall and break all kinds of bones. But now that Ben had given her a new angle on things, Laney said she guessed she could get some pads like the kids use and go for it in her fourth decade of life.

She figured her dear animal companion would like that. He could sit in his wheelbarrow and listen for this, she chuckled, old 70s veteran take to the concrete. That was one way to age gracefully. And she and Ben could do it together.

Finishing her notes on Ben and Laney that evening, Sharon considered the mirroring gift the elderly dog had given to his human companion. Its sweet simplicity transported her to a passage from a book that was itself a long timer on her bookshelf. In *The Velveteen Rabbit*, the aging rabbit reminds the reader of the ultimate grace in moving forward in time: "He even began to lose his shape, and he scarcely looked like a rabbit anymore, except to the Boy. To him, he was always beautiful and that was all that the little Rabbit cared about."

Ben, the Brittany Spaniel.

17

LOSS AND GRIEF

*He found himself listening for something. It
was the sound of the yearling for which he
listened, running around the house or stirring
on his moss pallet in the corner of the bedroom.
He would never hear him again. . . . Flag—He
did not believe he should ever again love
anything, man or woman or his own child,
as he had loved the yearling.*

The Yearling, Marjorie Rawlings

With the last of her comments recorded in the client files, Sharon closed the drawer of the metal cabinet, grabbed a tattered book off the shelf and stepped outside to join Lily. Sitting next to her feline friend on the porch stoop, the animal intuitive closed her eyes and inhaled Mt. Shasta's temperate summer air. Soothed by the perfume from the nearby lilac bush, she thought about the day's sessions. Three lingered with her. Not because the readings were unusual, but indeed, just the opposite, because the stories of Cavalier, Shadow and Princess were so movingly familiar.

Of the hundreds of consultations she had provided since she'd begun her work, the majority of the calls were from people dealing with the impending or recent loss of an animal companion, as well as the profound grief that ensued. Whether the loss and grief were from disappearance or death, all who sought the animal communicator's help expressed a common experience: raw, their hearts were being shredded.

Without a doubt, Sharon understood that kind of sorrow. Had she not felt the slashing pain of loss with her father's suicide, her daughter's disappearance and her beloved animal companion Shoji's sudden death? Yet, through those agonizing experiences she had come to know something else, something that the animals had communicated to her repeatedly, something that she continues to pass along to others: acknowledge and feel the painful loss, but in dealing with the heartache, embrace trust. Trust that not only is everything going to be all right, both for the one whom you've "lost" and for the one remaining on earth—you—but also trust that although the physical passes away, love does not. For the spirit of a being or of a genuine relationship is forever etched into the Universe.

In their service to humankind, animals (not only as true companions but also as faithful mirrors) reflect this universal wisdom. Certainly Cavalier the cat, Shadow the dog, and Princess the horse had presented this truth to their human partners with three different departures: disappearance, a natural death, euthanasia with honor.

As summer's unhurried twilight descended on her and Lily, Sharon recalled their stories.

∗   ∗   ∗

Crisp in its new exterior colors, the house was no longer a project in progress but a finished beauty that made Maddie proud. Waving goodbye to the painters who had been at her Pennsylvania home for the past three weeks, the copper-haired woman watched the crew drive away.

With the homeplace returning to its undisturbed milieu, she quickly headed for the back door. She wanted to alert Cavie that the coast was clear for his exit. Inside the house since early morning, the feline bounded onto the backyard. The change in the daily agenda and the workers' frequent presence had taken its toll on the cat, a sensitive creature who didn't do well with change. He was most content when life purred along with an unaltered routine.

Though there was one other variable to factor into maintaining Cavalier's equilibrium: his need to be near Maddie and Phillip, Maddie's husband. And it had been that way for their animal companion from the day he first curled into their laps.

Seven years ago, driving from North Carolina to Massachusetts, the couple had pulled into a restaurant parking lot in search of a take-out supper. As Maddie went inside to order, Phillip stretched his legs, then checked the car's condition.

Unbeknownst to the man, a bedraggled cat checked *him* out from the bushes and soon attempted an introduction. With a bloodied tail and uneven steps, the feline boldly approached Phillip. Gently lifting the injured cat, Phillip placed him in his lap. Without resistance, the tabby settled in and when Maddie returned, he easily sought her lap. Naming him Cavalier for his bravery, or Cavie for short, the couple took him to their motel room, cleaned his wounds and gave the famished cat a hearty supper.

Completing their vacation with Cavie, Maddie and Phillip welcomed him to their family. In time, the bond between the three mushroomed. As their animal companion, Cavalier took his role seriously. When Phillip required months to recover from a car accident, Cavie was by his side. When Maddie found herself doubting her own abilities, from the practical to the spiritual, Cavie was by her side.

During this time, with her dedicated assistant trailing at her feet, Maddie would often stop, bend down and gather her partner in her arms. Nuzzling her face into his soft belly, she'd tell the feline how much she loved him.

Though Cavie was secure in the company of Maddie and Phillip, it would take several years for the once-homeless and battered animal to feel entirely at ease with his environment. Unexpected noises (such as water from the shower or an unfamiliar person's voice) and unanticipated movements (even the stride of Phillip's feet) could send Cavalier into an anxiety attack.

But one of his biggest apprehensions came with the sight of Phillip pulling a suitcase out of the closet. With his career back on track and requiring frequent travel, Phillip was often away from home. Over the last few months, as Phillip packed, Cavie would jump into the bag and urinate, as if to stamp his disapproval for his human friend leaving again.

Though she understood its necessity, Maddie too dreaded her husband's absences. And with the recent miscarriage of their first pregnancy, she seemed to be more emotional about each business trip. Cavie's spraying, not only in the suitcases but also at times around the house, only added to her irritability.

Looking for answers to her animal companion's sporadic squirting, Maddie took Cavie to Dr. Bob Goldstein for a full exam. But the veterinarian could find no physical abnormalities to attribute the cat's behaviors to. Suggesting she contact an animal intuitive who specialized in animal communication, the doctor gave Maddie the Web site address for Sharon Callahan. That night she emailed the animal communicator for a consultation.

Already three months out with appointments, Sharon replied that she would send Cavalier a flower essence for him to take until their scheduled session. Derived from Mt. Shasta's vibrant wildflowers, Windflower would help even his emotions. "Inappropriate spraying," she noted, "is an emotional response to fear. All kinds of fear, especially fear of changes." In her email, Sharon also suggested that Maddie put up a progress chart at Cavalier's eye level. Her marking the visual graph was critical, the anxious cat communicated to Sharon. Using gold stars, Maddie was to put one up on the calendar every day he didn't urinate indiscriminately around the house. Also, Maddie might want to consider acknowledging some of her own fears, as animal companions, she explained, often mirror their human partner's emotional issues.

Eight weeks later, watching Cavie race for the bushes near the fence, Maddie sat on the deck and thought not only how the feline's fearful behaviors had already lessened but also how her own frustration with them had waned. The star-reward calendar she'd caught him looking at more than once had apparently played a role in his improvement. Perhaps her commitment to face her own angst honestly had helped, too.

As if to confirm her observations, the spry cat popped his head out of the bushes and, with his golden feline eyes, looked directly at Maddie. Locking into his brief stare, she felt a trusting and loving resonance she couldn't define. As he turned away to go on his regular rounds, she experienced a strange desire to rush to him, scoop him up in her arms and hold on to him forever. But she dismissed the fearful thought, as she observed him slip adventurously back into the hedge and move out from the house.

Calling for her animal companion to come in for the night a few hours later to sleep with them as he always did, Maddie had no response.

But it was summer time and with Cavie's love for the outdoors, she stifled her concern.

The next morning, however, brought no sign of Cavalier. Trying not to be swallowed up by fearful thoughts, she searched the neighborhood. Her voice hoarse from calling Cavie's name, and her eyes burning from a cascade of tears, she frantically knocked on doors and combed the streets and alleyways until nightfall. No Cavie.

Before falling into bed, she e-mailed Sharon Callahan about Cavalier's disappearance, asking if the animal intuitive could direct her in the search. Maddie knew it might be awhile before Sharon could answer, but she, afraid of the worst scenario, was getting desperate.

The following day she targeted the nearby hills. Stomping through the brush, she scoured the terrain, as the sun and clouds played hopscotch overhead. Her heart played the same game with every near sighting and near sound she had. Yet each time no tangerine feline appeared. By late afternoon, however, other animals did.

Overhead a bald eagle circled several times, then finally headed west. A heron dipped repeatedly toward her in a soothing swirl. A rabbit, scurrying across her path, halted for a moment, and giving her his full attention, seemed to offer solace.

But it was the mother and the baby who snagged Maddie's attention the most late that afternoon. Poised, a doe and her fawn headed uphill for a stream and walked unabashedly by her. If Maddie had extended her arm, she could almost have touched them. A few yards past her, the baby deer stopped and lay down in the shrubs hidden from view. Feeling as if the fawn had something for her, Maddie waited as her heart beat loudly—so loudly that she hoped the sound wouldn't scare the deer away. Realizing that she was afraid—not of the deer, but of what she wasn't sure—Maddie asked the camouflaged deer if he had a message for her.

In an instant she felt the deer's reply as surely as if the fawn had spoken audibly to her: Cavie wants you to stop looking for him. There's no need. Though he's no longer in his body, he's still close to you. Just as you can't see me, yet I'm here, it is the same with Cavie. With that, the baby deer clambered from the thicket and ran uphill to his mother.

Running downhill, Maddie headed toward home with her mind a jumble. Had she imagined the message from the wild creature? Had Cavie really passed on? How would she live without him? What could she trust? Catching her breath in her backyard, Maddie sat down in a lawn chair and sobbed.

An hour later, her eyes bloodshot, her body limp, Maddie sat down in front of her computer. Online, she checked her email. Sharon had replied. She had a cancellation that night at 8:00; she would book Maddie for that time.

Explaining the events of the day, along with her own confusion and grief over Cavalier's disappearance, Maddie began the telephone session with the animal intuitive. She wanted to know if her precious animal companion was okay, if the fawn had really given her a message from Cavie, and if so, if she'd understood it correctly.

As Sharon slipped into Cavie's energy, the cat communicated to her with feelings, visual images and thought transfers. Confirming that the deer was correct, he had passed over, the feline said he'd been chased and fatally attacked in an unfamiliar area and couldn't make it back home. But he'd decided to face his fears and, as a mirror for Maddie, help her face hers.

As they both were afraid of being separated from those they cherished, the experience offered them a chance to not only confront that fear, but also the opportunity to welcome its antidote: trust. With trust, they could see the big picture: that life was unfolding as it should be; that he and Maddie would always be together in spirit; and, most importantly, that love is beyond the shears of death.

Communicating those final messages to Maddie, Sharon concluded the session with Cavalier. Across the continent, Maddie thanked them both, her eyes awash with tears. She did, however, have one more question for Sharon. She wanted to know where she could find Cavie's body. She'd hoped to not only touch her boy again but also to give him a proper burial.

Though she understood that Maddie, like most people, had the need for concrete closure, Sharon gently suggested that Maddie relinquish the necessity to locate her animal companion's body. Not everything that occurs in life can draw to a close with a rational resolution, especially when it comes to loss and grief, she added. But those incomplete endings can be gifts in their own way. As Cavie pointed out, they can be catalysts for a spiritual renaissance, if one remembers the remedy for all sorrow: trust.

Cavalier, the cat who learned to face his fears.

As she lay in bed that night, she could almost feel Cavalier's warm body at her feet. But she knew the real warmth was coming from his presence in her heart. Though there was no doubt she was going to miss her animal companion for awhile, she really was beginning to trust that he hadn't really gone anywhere. For she knew his love was with her at all times.

*   *   *

Slowing inching the car forward, Cliff pulled into the garage. With the motor silent, he turned to look at his wife June. Unable to go through with their plans to have the vet put Shadow down, they were now back home. Without a word, the couple turned to look at their animal companion in the back seat.

Moving laboriously, the elderly dog, whose body was laced with arthritis, attempted to lift herself up. Peering out the window at the familiar surroundings, she was happy to be home, but without assistance, the 16-year-old Shetland Sheepdog couldn't get out of the vehicle.

As Cliff carried Shadow inside the house, June thought back to how the canine acquired her name. Given to their then eight-year-old son who was having problems in school, Shadow immediately bonded with the sensitive child. Whether greeting Rick at the driveway as the school bus let him off, or lying beside him as he slept, Shadow was indeed the boy's shadow. When Rick dubbed the dog *Shadow*, everyone in the family, even his two older brothers, agreed that the name was perfect.

For the next 10 years, Shadow was there for their son. With her soft, gentle eyes and her playful ways, the steadfast dog not only encouraged Rick's self-worth, but she also encouraged his laughter. And Shadow wasn't miserly with her gifts of unflagging companionship; she gave freely to everyone in the household.

Once all the children were out of the house and on their own, and Cliff's occasional out-of-state work left them alone, Shadow became June's shadow. Accompanying her ever-busy human partner throughout the day, the canine buddy lent her support with various projects around the home. Including mentoring the family's two new animal companions, the Great Pyrenees Niki and Katie.

But her first allegiance was to June. And when it came to overseeing the building of her and Cliff's new home, Shadow was there, too. Following June on her frequent progress checks during construction, the Sheltie would indicate her favorite areas. The garage space and the back yard seemed to always get her hip-shaking, happy-jumping approval.

When the couple moved into their dream house, however, they noticed a change in Shadow. Now nearing her 15th year, the senior canine was becoming stiff and slow in her movements. In months, arthritis's stranglehold became more blatant. Staying close to June became a demanding exercise for the faithful dog, but her allegiance kept her sore body moving.

By Shadow's birthday, her mobility declined even further. No longer able to stand, much less walk, the 60-pound Sheltie was bedridden. But that didn't deter June from keeping her animal companion involved in life. Pulling a blanketed Shadow around in a red wagon, thanks to the ramp Cliff built to the garage and into the house hallway, she and the Sheltie continued their routines. Sometimes, though, June felt as if Shadow, hanging her head low, her moist eyes shuttered by her eyelids, seemed almost apologetic about her condition. But June would stroke the dog with the touch of her hand, as well as with the words of loving assurance that the two of them were in this for the long haul. No pun, intended, she'd add with a hug.

Through a friend, June learned about an animal communicator on the West Coast. Scheduling a session, she hoped to gain some insights for dealing with Shadow's aging condition.

Pointing out that dogs over time become very much like people, more so than other animals, Sharon, in the reading, explained that domestic canines could suffer from all the same emotional tugs that humans do. And when they're elderly they will worry, just as people do, about what will happen to them when they can no longer get around and what will happen if they begin to make a mess.

But there were things June could do or, as in June's case continue to do, the animal intuitive informed the woman in Tennessee. She should keep Shadow comfortable; she should strive to strengthen Shadow's energy reserves as much as possible by never stressing her physical, emotional and mental energy beyond her limits; and, of course, she should dispense abundant love daily. And June could pay attention to all that Shadow showed her every day, for often it shone beyond the most apparent.

Merging with the feeble dog, the animal intuitive communicated with Shadow via emotions that were translated into words. She expressed to Sharon that although her bodily movements were leashed, her desire to serve June had not been. As her animal companion, the Sheltie still took special pride in being with her human friend and, as a mirror to June's soul, she wasn't ready to retire just yet.

When June asked about the mirror aspect, the animal intuitive explained that in service to their human companions, animals often reflect people's behaviors and needs back to them for their soul's attention. This reflection can help their people friends grow in spirit and in truth. As your mirror, Shadow's actions and requirements today are teaching you, Sharon pointed out, to slow down, to be fully present in the moment and to cherish life as it is today.

With Shadow's 16th birthday, the bond between June and Shadow had welded even tighter. Lugging her animal companion from place to place, lifting her up and taking her outside to eliminate, and keeping her healthy with the best food and nutritional supplements, demanded much of June's time both day and night. Though exhausted, those necessities she could handle. What she couldn't handle was seeing Shadow so bound by the arthritis. Certainly, the flower essence had helped Shadow's moods and soothed her discomfort, but nothing could slow down time. Aging was a part of being on this planet; she knew that firsthand.

But sometimes, late into the night, when she was awakened by Shadow's bark alert that she needed to urinate and would go to the arthritic dog, June wondered if maybe Shadow were beyond mere discomfort and suffering greatly. Perhaps, she should even be put to sleep. Well-intentioned friends, including Shadow's veterinarian, and neighbors had urged June and Cliff to put their animal partner out of her misery. Some even hinted that the couple was being uncaring by letting the dog live.

But they didn't feel that way. At least most of the time. After Shadow experienced several "bad" days in a row, however, she and Cliff reversed their earlier decision. They decided to go to the vet and have their beloved animal companion euthanized. Although she'd wanted to wait for an upcoming reading she had with the animal communicator, June realized that she couldn't bear for Shadow to go through another day in her debilitating condition.

Yet, she was torn, too. A part of her felt it was the right thing to do, yet a part of her felt it wasn't right to euthanize her animal friend. The latter won out when she and Cliff drove past the veterinary clinic without stopping and returned home with a very sentient Shadow still with them.

During another scheduled session the following week, June asked Sharon what she should do about her dear animal companion. Merging with the feeble dog, the animal intuitive communicated that Shadow first wanted to let June know that although her body was sore and moving was difficult, she was in no real pain and was not suffering. Second, and most important, she wanted to thank Cliff and June for not having her put to sleep. Shadow said that when it was her time, she wanted to die naturally at home, around all that she loved.

Elaborating, the canine said that animals prefer to experience a natural death. With this normal ebb in the cycle of life, there is a more flowing transition. An ending that is abrupt and chosen by another goes against the rhythm of the body. Though there are times when leaving the physical body by intervention is acceptable, it is to be used only in extreme situations. Shadow said she and all animals wished not only to be allowed to reap the full benefits of the earth-time experience but also to have their exits treated with reverence.

Interrupting Sharon, June asked if there was anything she could do to make the last days better for her friend. Communicating through the animal intuitive, the dog replied with several requests.

Preferring to smell the air outside and see nature's landscape, she wanted to be moved to the garage, under the couple's bedroom. As her favorite color was electric blue, she'd like it if June could make a tent out of that color for her. She asked that the tent's door and the garage door be left half open. That way she, wrapped in her blankets, could view her treasured backyard.

Shadow also requested that life in the household go on in a regular fashion, full of love and full of life. She still hoped to join June with the spring gardening duties, if June didn't mind hoisting her and placing her in the red wagon. She knew that took a lot out of June, but she also knew that at least they could still do that routine together. For, Shadow acknowledged, routine was now even more comforting and sweet in its familiarity than ever.

Addressing Sharon, June responded that with all the love and support the dog had bestowed upon the family over the years, and especially to her since the children were gone, June would be pleased to reciprocate in the coming days.

Shadow's final wish that she communicated to the animal intuitive centered on the time following her passing. She asked that June and Cliff resist the impulse to hold on or to grieve excessively. Shedding tears and missing her physical presence would indeed be an understandable and appreciated expression of loss and grief, but to hang on doggedly to these feelings, the Sheltie pointed out, was of no benefit to anyone. Especially to her, the one crossing over. The best way to help her with the transition, Shadow offered, was to simply send her on her way with loving trust. That spiritual gift would take her far, while keeping her human companions near.

As the session ended, June asked the animal intuitive if there was a flower essence she could recommend for Shadow's last days. The Senior Formula Sharon had sent for Shadow a few months back had helped the aging, arthritic dog. Sharon replied that the flower essence Pearly Everlasting would be appropriate as it was beneficial in helping an animal release his feelings of responsibility and bonds to the earthly life, allowing him to transit peacefully. For June and her husband, Sharon offered an essence remedy to employ once Shadow had passed over.

Drummond's Anemone, a Mt. Shasta wildflower, would aid them in releasing their grief over the loss of their precious animal companion.

As Shadow requested, June and Cliff erected the electric blue tent, moved their animal companion to the garage and did their best to go about their daily activities—with a couple of exceptions.

Taking breaks from her work, June would often lie in the tent beside Shadow, looking out with her to the beauty of the backyard and the woods beyond. Sometimes June spoke words of encouragement and appreciation; sometimes she said nothing, knowing that words were not needed. Just to be able to look into Shadow's beautiful eyes, wells of liquid light that expressed their own language of love, was enough.

One night as June entered the vibrant blue tent, she brought along some special supplies. Anointing Shadow's head with holy water, June told her canine buddy how much she loved her and all that she'd shown her about life. With tears and smiles, she offered a prayer and more spoken gratitudes. Though it was just the two of them there, June felt as if they weren't alone. With the air full of compassionate energy, angels seemed to surround them.

Ending the ceremony with the biggest gift she could give Shadow, she assured the Sheltie that anytime she wanted to go, it was okay with her. Lying next to June, Shadow relaxed, as the two of them looked out at the starry night.

The next day, returning from some errands, June eased the car into the garage and felt her body stiffen. Shadow did not raise her head as she normally did when June drove in. When Cliff came out to meet his wife, she knew what had happened.

Shadow, the Shetland Sheepdog.

Cradling Shadow's still body, June wrapped her beloved dog in the blue cloth she'd favored so much. Lighting candles and healing ash, the couple set up a viewing for their animal companion. Keeping the garage door open, June wanted to let nature view her just as Shadow had so fondly viewed nature.

In the morning light, Cliff and June placed the Sheltie in the red wagon and took her to the woods, just below the house where Shadow would visit often. Katie and Niki followed. After Cliff dug the grave, the couple gently placed their beloved friend inside. Planting a rose bush on top of the site, along with two heart bushes to represent their love, they thanked Shadow for all that the dog had taught them about life and about death. Then they cried.

*   *   *

Jackie placed the CD in the player and turned the volume up. As the harp music floated through the barn, Princess, with her ears forward and her head slightly lowered, softly neighed. Smiling, Jackie walked back to her old riding buddy and resumed her position next to her. Only paces away, Jackie's parents, her sister and brother-in-law stood by, telling one another stories about the 40-year-old horse, born the same year as Jackie.

As their affectionate tales, punctuated by laughter and sighs, joined the sweet aroma of the hay, Jackie stroked Princess' nuzzle. In an effort to later recall every nuance of her animal companion's body, she stepped back and took in Princess' endearing physical characteristics: her small, brown equine build of 14 hands framed by an ebony mane, tail and four socks; her regal face emblazoned in the center with a white star; and her singular eyes, one blue and one brown that twinkled with wisdom and frequent humor.

All these familiar features defined a good friend with whom Jackie had shared much, beginning with the season she'd first learned to ride. Whispering to Princess, Jackie reminded her pal of that summer when the horse taught her life's fundamentals—partnership and trust—through the ups and downs of horseback riding.

As a bratty 10-year-old, Jackie thought then that she was going to be the one in control as she plopped smugly aboard Princess. But the astute mare, with no tolerance for a bad attitude and strong hind legs for appropriate bucking, soon put the smart-alecky kid in her place: on the ground.

As summer progressed, however, and Jackie began to understand the dynamics of working closely together with her equestrian mentor, she was spending more time in the saddle than out. By autumn, the relationship between her and Princess had blossomed into one that resonated with respect, patience and genuine friendship. One that would mount the occasional separations Jackie's career later demanded and one that would bring them back together for one final juncture.

That meeting was today. With an untreatable hoof infection that no amount of antibiotics or hoof soaking could help, Princess was going to be put down. Unable to support her weight or to live without unrelenting pain, the elderly horse stood with the family with the aid of a temporary nerve block, which the vet had given her earlier, ready for the event. But this was not going to be an occasion orchestrated by the humans who loved her, though everyone in the barn was there to play a vital role. Instead, Princess' sacred exit was going to be on her own terms. Princess had assured Jackie of that months before she'd contracted the foot infection.

Living in San Francisco, 120 miles away from the family farm where Princess stayed, didn't allow Jackie to see her animal friend as often as she would have liked. Last autumn, eager to get an overview on Princess' well-being, Jackie had a telephone session with an animal intuitive to whom she'd been referred.

As she merged with Princess, Sharon Callahan informed Jackie that her animal companion was communicating with a waterfall of information. From sensory images to direct thoughts to visual graphics, connecting to the horse, the animal intuitive said, was like talking to a human. The only difference being that Princess didn't form auditory words.

Sharon's observation of Princess' communication skills didn't surprise Jackie. One of the reasons, she told Sharon, she felt so close to Princess was her horse's surreal ability to seemingly detect the full picture intellectually and emotionally of every situation.

The other was that their friendship required no words. For, like all good friends, they were on the same wavelength when they were together. Even when she no longer rode Princess because of the horse's age, Jackie said she was content to just be in the pasture with her horse.

Concurring with Jackie, Princess communicated that she was indeed intricately connected to her human friend. Yet, there were some things she wanted to make sure Jackie understood.

First, she wanted to thank her for allowing her to retire. Most of her species didn't have that joy. Many times when horses grow older, are failing or are no longer useful, they are dispensed with. Some end up in rendering plants. She was grateful to have been *truly* put out to pasture.

Second, Princess told Sharon that when it was her time to go, she wanted certain arrangements to be made. She wanted the family to be around, laughing and talking of the good times; she wanted heavenly music to abound; and she wanted to be buried in the pasture. She would show Jackie where the next time she came to the farm.

Third, as Jackie's mirror, the horse said it was her responsibility to show her human friend her inner strengths as well as her drawbacks. By reflecting those traits, Princess said she could help Jackie grow in spirit.

Jackie's Herculean qualities, Princess relayed, were her kindness and her patience. Though, she added humorously, she might take some credit in helping a young Jackie acquire that latter quality 30 years ago. Jackie's Achilles' heel was her lack of trust in herself. By not trusting her inner guidance and her own abilities, she often tripped over life's demands. But, Princess added, Jackie would have an opportunity to confront that obstacle again soon. This time, she knew her human companion would clear the hurdle with finesse.

As the consultation neared its conclusion, Sharon explained to Jackie the relevance of animal companions in people's lives. Just as Princess had alluded to, they are not only beloved companions and friends, she said that they are also mirrors reflecting important truths back to their human friends. Paying attention to those truths can be beneficial to maintaining emotional and spiritual harmony.

A few days ago, when Jackie received word that Princess was failing and certain decisions needed to be made regarding the horse, she thought back to the reading, when Princess predicted that Jackie would soon have to confront an obstacle head-on.

That *soon* had galloped into Jackie's life more quickly and in quite a different scenario than she had expected. Always figuring that Princess would die a natural death, she found it unreal to conceive otherwise. Yet, aware that her comrade was still teaching her about life, Jackie had to concede in some ways, it made, well, horse sense.

Princess' current scenario, after all, had set her up to deal with some major life issues. With having to make the critical decision about her long-time equine friend's well-being, Jackie had to face self-doubt.

With having to eventually endure Princess' departure, she'd have to face the jagged ice pick of loss and grief.

Walking with Princess in the pasture yesterday afternoon was the first step in dealing with both. With the first of three painkillers that would take her through the next 24 hours, Princess slowly guided Jackie to a knoll in the field. Stopping, she looked out over the vista, then at her human friend. The serene, yet very-present horse lowered her head, placing her nose on the ground. The spot, Jackie noticed, sported a large matted-grass circle, obviously indented by constant use. As if to confirm Jackie's realization, Princess lay down in the sweet-smelling alfalfa. Aware that Princess had not only taken her to her favorite resting place, but also her final resting place, Jackie sat down beside her animal companion. Softly crying, her heart breaking, Jackie nuzzled Princess as Princess returned the gesture.

Not wishing to break their union, but understanding that time cannot remain idle for long, Jackie motioned for her sister and her brother-in-law to bring the excavator. After her brother-in-law dug the burial plot, the women spread hay into the hole. Once the grave was finished, Princess inspected the cavity carefully, then gently butted Jackie. The site was ready.

And now, as the time for the euthanasia approached, Jackie hoped she was ready. Not wanting to let her animal companion down, she aimed to be. Along with her family and the veterinarian, she laughed and added to the pool of Princess stories some her of treasured memories.

As she finished telling a memorable incident and her parents offered one of theirs, Jackie thought back to the conversation she had earlier in the morning with Sharon Callahan. Although the animal intuitive said that she believed in the sanctity of allowing animals going through the process of a natural death, she knew there were times when this was not possible. But the main objective in dealing with all transitions is that the animal be treated with honor.

Congratulating Jackie on her efforts to treat Princess' passing in this sacred manner, Sharon said that Princess communicated that she was also pleased with the process. With the family around and the music touching them all, she felt content.

She did, however, have just one last request: when the injection was given, she asked that no one hold his or her breath! Instead, Princess said that she'd rather everyone just laugh and send her on with good energy. Laughing and weeping at once, Jackie pledged that she would do just that when the time approached.

As if on cue, Princess interrupted Jackie's thoughts and walked over to the vet. As the veterinarian turned to retrieve the hypodermic syringe, everyone in the barn gave a loving caress to the brown horse. When the thiopentathal was injected, all, save for the harp music, was silent. But, remembering Princess' wishes, Jackie inhaled a sweet horse smell from her animal companion's coat deeply and began another Princess story. A funny one.

Showered by the laughter, Princess stood still for several minutes, to the amazement of the vet who had given her a large amount of the drug, then lay down for good. For the next 45 minutes, the family stayed with her, as more Princess tales filled the barn.

Jackie's old friend was then taken to her chosen grave and placed inside the hay-lined tomb. Clipping a piece of Princess' mane and braiding it, the vet handed Jackie the keepsake. It would go next to a picture of Princess propped up on her bedside table.

Princess, the small bay mare.

In a final gesture of love, a misty-eyed Jackie placed a blanket from their early days together over Princess, as she thanked her animal companion for the riding lessons. Both those she learned on the beloved horse's back and those she learned by riding life's ups and downs with such a good friend. They, like Princess, would stay with her forever.

*   *   *

Opening the worn book in her lap, Sharon's thoughts drifted from Princess, Shadow and Cavalier to another story of grief and loss. One that expressed with simple eloquence the deep bond between a human and an animal companion. As her feline partner Lily slipped into her lap, Sharon read the words that could still move her heart. The passage was from Marjorie Rawling's *The Yearling*: "He found himself listening for something. It was the sound of the yearling for which he listened, running around the house or stirring on his moss pallet in the corner of the bedroom. He would never hear him again . . . Flag—He did not believe he should ever again love anything, man or woman or his own child, as he had loved the yearling."

18

LIGHTEN UP

"I didn't know Cheshire cats always grinned; in fact, I didn't know that cats could grin." "They all can," said the Duchess; "and most of 'em do." "I don't know of any that do," Alice said very politely, feeling quite pleased to have got into a conversation. "You don't know much," said the Duchess; "and that's a fact."

Alice's Adventures in Wonderland, Lewis Carroll

ashing into the animal clinic one humid Florida evening for some meds, Erin headed to the back exam room to talk to the veterinarian. She had only a moment, for she was impatient to return to her dying cat back home. But as she passed the entrance to the patients' holding area, she stopped and, as if being gently pulled forward by a magical leash, she edged toward a far corner cage. As Erin leaned in closer to see what was in the enclosure, the grinning face of a black and white cat popped up to greet her.

Before she could say something to the friendly feline, Dr. Mary came up behind her and tried to shoo Erin away. She warned her client and old friend not to look at the animal, no matter how charming she may appear. With two deformed kidneys that were untreatable, tomorrow she would be put down.

But when Erin protested that the cat was so good-natured and amiable, the vet agreed that she was indeed a charmer, but noted that didn't change the fact that she was dying. She said her owners had given her up, and, in the fatal shape the animal was in, the cat certainly wasn't a candidate for adoption.

She'd take her, Erin told the animal doctor. How could she, Mary wanted to know, when Erin was already nursing a sick cat. Miss Kitty, Erin's 20-year-old beloved feline was in her last days, and the costs of just trying to keep yet another animal's body functioning would not be pocket change, the vet warned. Plus Erin had two other cats at home who still took some extra attention at times.

With her finger inside the cage, now wet from the cat's stroking tongue, Erin turned back toward the vet and gave her a determined how-can-I-not smile.

Later, as she opened the carrier and the newcomer regally stepped onto the tiled kitchen floor, Erin knew what she would call the cat: Fiona. Without hesitation, Fiona, with head and tail held aloft, sauntered into the living room where Miss Kitty lay ill and tenderly spooned with the elderly feline. How strange, Erin thought, here's a cat that's dying herself, yet she faces death as if it were nothing to be afraid of.

Often, during the next three days, Erin would peek into the living room and observe Fiona in close communion with the lethargic Miss Kitty. More than once, as Erin watched Fiona place a scrawny paw on the senior cat, she found herself thinking that she wished she could be more like this fearless animal. Although she faithfully ministered to Miss Kitty's needs, Erin found it painful to truly accept the idea that her faithful cat, her first animal companion, was soon going to be gone.

The other cats in the house, staying clear of the living room, seemed to reflect those same feelings of denial. Even Ben, Fiona's husband who was often held hostage by his work anyway, found reasons to skirt the scene. But with Fiona, it was as if she had a different attitude toward death, and she was not about to hide that posture six feet under.

Once Miss Kitty passed a few days later, a chipper Fiona began acting out another lesson for the household: lighten up. Honor Miss Kitty—as well as all beings, including yourself—with the gift of lightness, appreciating not only the past with lighthearted memories, but also the beauty of the moment with a smile, or better yet, the persuasive powers of play.

From her crooked smile beep-beeps (roadrunner had nothing on her) to her unebbing efforts to entice the other cats to playfully stalk, chase, hide and chase again, Fiona was the quarterback of the game of living life with joy. Even Harley, a big tabby, who had come to Erin with a history of mistreatment and spent most of his days under the bed covers, was learning that play need not be an alien exercise. Sitting on his head until Harley would come after her, Fiona was determined that the boy get into the pleasurable habit of coming out to play.

Fiona was also benevolently pawing her way into Dharma's heart. The cat from hell, as one neighbor called him, was not labeled that because he was destructive, but because he was one bad-tempered creature. Another adoptee, Dharma had never known that the world could offer anything but meanness. But Fiona, the play maniac, altered that view with her intrepid attempts to rouse Dharma into a tag game. Before long, Dharma could be seen chasing Fiona and ending the game with a rolling party.

But Fiona required no play partner to have fun. Everything was a toy to this jocular creature: a bread bag twisty dropped on the floor was a hockey puck that begged to be shot across the room; a lid from a cooking pot was a noisy cymbal that had to be scratched. But her favorite activity was perching on the highest object in any room and, with her droll grin, waiting for the inevitable rescue attempt by Erin. Each time, thinking that this supposedly frail cat had climbed too far to safely descend, Erin would head for the garage for a ladder. But when she hurriedly returned to save the cat, dragging the heavy ladder, Fiona would adroitly and lightly drop down to the sofa, and stalk off with a spark in her eye so that Erin would know the joke was on her.

Even at the animal clinic, during the many blood transfusions Fiona required, the cat was a comedian. Batting at the doctors' stethoscopes, fiddling with the syringes and tubes as if they were toys, Fiona kept the normally somber procedures light and the staff in stitches. Even the other animals around seemed to be uplifted by the spirited cat.

In the waiting room, Erin would hear the laughs and the amazement that such an ill being could take such delight in entertaining them. Fiona was barely seven pounds, with few blood cells to carry oxygen, yet she brought life to everyone around her.

One afternoon, as Fiona was having yet another blood transfusion, Erin flipped through an animal magazine in the clinic's lounge. When her eyes landed on an article about an animal intuitive, she read and reread the information. According to Animal Intuitive Sharon Callahan, animal companions are in our lives for a purpose. That purpose is cradled in service. Serving as both a mirror and a mentor to their human companions, animals offer loving lessons in living a balanced and spiritually aware life.

Erin made an appointment. When she phoned Sharon, she told the animal communicator that she wanted to know about a cat whom she'd adopted called Fiona.

Merging with Fiona, Sharon felt the feline's gargantuan, lighthearted energy. Commenting that the cat radiated the kind of clownlike personality that was infectious, Sharon immediately connected with Fiona's thoughts and mental pictures. Sharon told Erin that Fiona communicated with vibrant visual messages. Animals with a great enthusiasm for life and a great sense of humor, like Fiona, often express themselves well mentally. Like humans, they, too, can be witty.

Fiona told Erin that she had been waiting for her that day at the vet's office. She entered Erin's life to serve by example. By mirroring, the cat would teach her two things. One was to learn how to not take life—and even death—so seriously; the other was to learn how, when life did hand you a stinker, to perfume the situation with a good dose of humor.

In response, Erin acknowledged that she did have problems dealing with loss. With the recent pain of Miss Kitty's death, she was now afraid of losing Fiona. With the feline's kidney illness, she knew it could be sooner instead of later.

As a child, she had never been allowed to have an animal companion. Her father, thinking he was protecting her, said he didn't want one to die on her, for it was a devastatingly painful thing to endure. His warning had stayed with her.

But it was another childhood memory that still weighed her heart down like a bag full of stones. When she was 11 years old, a dam broke behind her home, destroying it. Though no family members were killed, there was a death of sorts: a loss of security, faith and, with no insurance to replace their belongings, self-esteem. Struggling to survive, the family began again, each day an unrelenting, hard effort to get things done. Joy had died and so had the notion of play. Work became the family's mantra. And, though today she was blessed with financial security, she knew she still followed that all-work-and-no-time-for-play ideology.

Then there was Ben. A computer software engineer, her husband was a meticulous, detail-oriented man who was in constant demand at work. From his involved presentations to his long office hours, she didn't think he knew what fun was either.

But he was going to see the light, Fiona communicated to Sharon, because, like a reliable mirror, she was going to reflect it to him. Just as she was demonstrating to Erin, Dharma and Harley, Fiona was going to teach them all—and not just scratch the surface—the gravity of having play in their lives. With this remark, Fiona projected scenes of her daredevil jumping off Erin's rescue ladder onto the sofa below.

Giggling over the comment and the image Sharon shared with Erin, the two women agreed that this was one sassy cat. The message that Fiona wanted Erin to take home with her today was this: take time to look around you and find some fun. Toss out the frustrations, disappointments and the boredom enveloping you, and dive deeply into life's toy box to retrieve a bit of fun you can play in the moment.

Over the next few months, between medical treatments, Fiona kept her promise to show them all the way to the toy box—beginning with Ben. That night, after the reading with Sharon, Erin conveyed to her husband their cat's concerns about him. Expecting this logical, analytical man to dismiss her, Erin was pleasantly taken aback when the misty-eyed Ben agreed with Fiona's assessment. He did need to enjoy life more. But he said he did have some work to do first.

In his home office, as he began refining a computer presentation, an idea, wild and furry, sprang into his normally sober mind. Opening the desk drawer, he grabbed the laser pointer and returned to the kitchen where Fiona was lapping up the last of her supper.

Facing the wall, he directed the marker here, there and everywhere. It wouldn't take long, he suspected, before the king, no, queen of the jungle would roar. Abruptly, from out of the ethers, a creature jumped up in front of the projected screen, aiming for the laser light. No matter where Ben put the red glow, an outstretched paw connected to a manically goofy cat tried to capture the crimson beam. At first bemused and then belly laughing, Ben was soon playing the bet-you-can't-get-it game with Fiona.

Taking the challenge around the kitchen, Ben soon had the high-spirited feline knocking over everything to catch that speedy light. But whether she nabbed it, sat on it or even laid on it, the red light had a way of scooting out of her grasp.

Ben's howls brought Erin running to the room, where she joined in on the fun with her husband. After that, the red-dot laser game became a regular event.

But Fiona's efforts to seduce her family into play didn't stop there. One of her favorite diversions was hide-and-go-seek. Disappearing into the linen and clothes closet, the silly cat would emit eerie noises, like a ship foghorn warning, in hopes of being found. Once Erin would find her, the chase was on. If her human companion said she didn't have time to play this game, Fiona only secured another hiding place to sound the foghorn.

Accompanied by her human companion, Fiona was also ecstatic about taking excursions outside while adorned with her red (no way she was going to wear the blue or black) necklace (*necklace* was to be used instead of *leash* she had told Sharon) to chase some willing lizards.

Six months after Erin's first consultation with Sharon, Erin spoke again to the animal intuitive. She told Sharon that she was learning a lot looking carefully at Fiona's reflections of the good life. Erin admitted she still had plenty to assimilate, but she was more open now.

Already, she was seeing play in a different way. No longer irritated or calling people who took time off irresponsible, Erin said Fiona's promise to show them how to lighten up was working.

As for Fiona herself, her physical health was holding up; she still amazed the health care providers. Not only with her stamina and courage, but also, there was no doubt about it, with her flair for comedy.

Later, penning notes in Fiona's file, Sharon pondered the *lighten-up* message the cat had given to all those around her. It was some astute advice that could benefit us all. Facing the world each day with a grin was some good medicine.

A grin. Her thoughts floated to a passage from a childhood book. Still a part of her hardback collection, the book rested on the office bookcase shelf. Walking over to the worn copy, she withdrew *Alice's*

Adventures in Wonderland and filtered through the pages. Immediately, she found the words that she was searching for, words that so aptly described Fiona. Indeed, the optimistic feline was the living embodiment of the Cheshire cat who played the best game of all: the grinning game. Out loud, with a growing smile on her own face, Sharon read:

> "I didn't know Cheshire cats always grinned; in fact, I didn't know that cats could grin."
> "They all can," said the Duchess; "and most of 'em do."
> "I don't know of any that do," Alice said very politely, feeling quite pleased to have got into a conversation.
> "You don't know much," said the Duchess; "and that's a fact."

Fiona, the cat.

19

ON BEING DIFFERENT

He was very happy, but not at all proud, for a
good heart never becomes proud. He thought of
how he had been pursued and scorned, and
now he heard them all say that he was the
most beautiful of all beautiful birds.

The Ugly Duckling, Hans Christian Andersen

On a **Web** site featuring adoptive animals, a Great Dane with natural, uncropped ears, caught the eye of Jewel. Reading the bio about Blue, the woman noticed that the 14-month-old dog was different in another way. With a flap of furry skin covering a missing right eye, along with an intact left eye that did not function, the Great Dane was blind. Identified as a special needs dog, the canine would require much from her adoptive human family, the site noted.

Though Jewel already had two dogs, Kurvenal, a Great Dane, and Casey, a Labrador Retriever, something about this creature grabbed at her. And it had nothing to do with pity; instead, it had everything to do with connecting with the dog on a very visceral level. She knew she had to have her, even though she'd had no plans of adopting another dog that night. She had been, after all, just browsing the site.

Within an hour, she was on the phone to the listed foster home, setting up a Sunday afternoon appointment to meet the Great Dane. Fortunately, the couple lived only a 45-minute drive from Jewel's Chicago home. But before she would go, she would talk to Sharon Callahan, an animal intuitive whose communication skills with animals had helped Jewel out many times with understanding her dogs, and she knew, at times, with herself.

During the Saturday session, set up before she'd come across Blue, Jewel asked Sharon if Kurvenal and Casey would mind if the dog joined the family. Both animal companions responded that it was okay with them, though they did want to go with Jewel to pick up the Great Dane. Sharon added that the new dog wanted to request something. Communicating through a direct transfer of thoughts, she said she'd prefer that her name not be Blue but something more sparkling in that hue: Sapphire. Sharon noted that sapphire was a significant choice as, according to legend, the gemstone possessed powerful wisdom that provided positive solutions to challenging obstacles. Jewel agreed to dub her Sapphire.

The next day, as she walked into the area where Sapphire was staying, Jewel knew at first sight that this was a special being. But what Sapphire *saw*, well, Jewell wondered about that. For though she understood the dog could actually see nothing in a purely physical sense, she marveled at how so completely at ease with her surroundings, even with the two unfamiliar dogs around her, the Great Dane (weighing less than 100 pounds and standing only 32 inches tall, she was actually a small one) seemed.

Once home, the family of three dogs and Jewel, a shy, professional woman in her late 40s, settled in, sort of. Relying on auditory cues, she soon figured out how to handle Sapphire's blindness. For Kurvenal, it took about a month for him to realize that the newest family member wasn't ignoring him when she failed to respond to familiar, or what should have been familiar, canine sight signals. He, too, began using sound cues instead with her and soon began to interact more easily with his fellow Great Dane. Within eight months, however, both he and Casey had passed, making way eventually for Nicholas, a Lab mix, and Hamlet, a Great Dane/Mastiff mix.

The latter adoptee, never having been in a house, had much to learn. Hoping to help with this, Jewel enrolled Hamlet in an obedience class. Practicing commands and exercises with the dog, Jewel noticed that Sapphire kept attempting to be a part of the activities. It was as if she not only wanted to be challenged but also wanted to demonstrate that she, too, could do what was asked of her. Already, the Great Dane, for her own daily survival and enjoyment, could respond to such commands as *left* (turn left), *right* (turn right), *step* (step over something) and *careful* (a warning to her that she was coming up to an object).

Before she took Sapphire out to a class, however, Jewel wanted to make sure her animal companion wished to go. In a session with Sharon, Sapphire told Jewel that she was not only ready to go, she was looking forward to the challenges. And she promised to be a good girl.

For weeks, Jewel sought a class that would agree to have a blind dog. Over and over again, Sapphire and she were denied access. Each time she would hang up the phone after hearing the customary litanies and sigh. She'd heard them all before: from "having a disabled dog in class might make others in the class uncomfortable" to "how can a dog without sight perform the exercise" to "it's just too much trouble." Nearby, Sapphire seemed to sigh in disappointment as well. During those times of discrimination and rejection, the dog would often go to bed without going through the obedience exercises that she normally looked forward to each night. Being different, her body seemed to say as she padded off to bed, could sometimes hurt.

Finally, one class begrudgingly agreed to accept them. But when Jewel walked in with Sapphire, she was glad that her animal companion couldn't see the looks thrown their way. They said quite plainly that the people in the room thought the situation with the woman and her blind dog couldn't possibly work. Not only would a visually impaired dog, who couldn't see the signals or the obstacles ahead, not be able to accurately follow commands, but her presence would slow everything down.

For a moment, Jewel hesitated. Ever a diffident and unassuming person, taking an overt stand on something, especially in front of a room full of strangers she didn't know, was intimidating. Not only was she not sure she could put Sapphire through this, but she also wasn't sure she could put herself through this. After all, Sapphire would be depending on her to lead the way. Literally. What if she messed up?

But she and Sapphire didn't. Using hand claps, Jewel communicated with her animal companion. Successfully completing each demand, from on-off leash recall to sit and stay to low jumps, Sapphire rose to the occasion. Outdoing most of the other dogs, she was one happy tail-wagging canine that day. It was also a good day for Jewel, not only because they had both met their challenges, but also because she'd learned about an organization where Sapphire would be welcomed as well as challenged.

Rally O, Rally obedience for all dogs, sponsored by the Association of Pet Dog Trainers, was a group that believed in teaching one's dog via mutual trust and respect. Working with them and participating in their trials would prove to be a long and satisfying association, though discrimination against one with differences can be found anywhere.

Before Sapphire's first obedience trial, Jewel enrolled them in a class to prepare for the competition. She learned there that she really needed to have more prep classes before the trial, but there was no time to take them all. Offering to help her along with the rules, and what could be modified for a disabled dog, the class instructor turned to a trial judge who happened to be nearby. Acting as if the two novices were wasting their time, the judge offered little encouragement to Jewel and Sapphire.

Later, in another class, they again met resistance but in an even more painful way. For it had nothing to do with the dog's abilities but with her appearance. Sitting on a bench next to a woman with a Lab, Jewel and her animal companion were waiting for the classroom to be ready for the class to enter. Making announcements, the instructor announced in a caring way that there was a special dog in the class and asked that all give consideration to Sapphire's movements, as with her blindness, she could not be expected to be aware of everyone and everything. Giving Sapphire and Jewel a nasty look, the woman with the Lab grabbed her dog's leash and, acting as if the Great Dane were defective, unfit and would contaminate her dog, hurried over to the other side of the room. Taken aback, Jewel patted Sapphire on the head, hoping that her beloved animal companion was not bitten by this unkind action.

A few days later, Jewel had a session with Sharon Callahan. Concerned that Sapphire was being hurt by the discrimination she often had to face and that she might be pushing her too hard, Jewel asked the animal intuitive to communicate with Sapphire.

Merging with the Great Dane, Sharon was able to pick up the dog's transfer of thoughts and something else: colorful, pulsating energy images. Sapphire pointed out that this is what she sees when she moves through a physical space; she sees the energy of it, for all things have a vibratory essence. These energy images, Sharon noted, were much like what people see when they see static on a TV screen, except much prettier.

Answering her human companion's queries, Sapphire communicated to Sharon that one of her jobs in life is helping people overcome their fear of those with handicaps. Yes, she was sensitive to people's negative reactions to her, but she was not sad for herself, she was sad for them, for their hearts were often closed down. For she didn't feel her blindness was a handicap as much as it was something that made her different in a good way. A blessing in disguise, being different can bring out parts of you that being normal doesn't demand. Not only do you learn to rely on other physical senses more acutely, such as hearing, taste and smell, but you become more aware of feelings, making you more sensitive to all life. When Jewel asked about the woman with the Labrador Retriever, Sapphire responded that it did indeed hurt a bit, but mostly it made her feel great compassion for them. For discrimination comes from ignorance and fear.

Jewel knows about this, Sapphire communicated. As a shy person, she's often discriminated against. Not in a mean way, but she's pushed aside socially as people do not know there is more to her than what her silence shows. With the two of them being rejected for class participations, she's also known another kind of discrimination. As her mirror, the animal companion said she hoped she'd reflected to her human partner how to stand her ground, for no matter what anyone's disability is, it's important to always move ahead with honor.

And as for Jewel's pushing Sapphire too hard, the dog relayed that she saw the competitions as fun and, more importantly, an opportunity to help other animals with disabilities as well as their human companions.

Though Sapphire's communication had quieted her doubts, Jewel was still nervous the day of the first trial. Aware that they hadn't taken the Rally O classes and that doing a wrong heel position would disqualify them, she felt a myriad of scary thoughts seeping through her confidence. And when she saw that one of the judges was the woman in the class who seemed to dismiss Sapphire's ability to perform the tasks of the trials, Jewel's edginess increased. But Sapphire, the only blind dog in the large room, seemed unfazed by her human friend's anxiety, mirroring to her a sense of solid faith.

Looking over the arena, Jewel saw at least a dozen (her stomach was too full of butterflies for her brain to count) different command signs dotting the course. The setup appeared to be very demanding for a big dog like Sapphire, especially when that big dog was also blind. Not only would a team have to follow the commands, but they also would have to do them exactly in order. Each human-and-dog team started off in the ring with 200 points, with the score being lowered when errors were made. The goal was to get 190 or over. Reaching that allowed the pair to get carrying points that moved them toward the obedience championships.

When their turn arrived, the two, with Sapphire's in-tune heeling and sitting, moved as one; even the 360-circle requirement and the figure eight around poles posed little challenge. Though, once because of her own neophyte moves, Jewel didn't give Sapphire her *careful* cue in time, and the dog narrowly avoided hitting the sign.

They ended up with a score of 179; but in the three other shows they participated in that day, they fetched scores over 190 each time. From then on, there seemed to be no obstacles the Sapphire-Jewel partnership couldn't overcome. And by the year 2004, Sapphire was ranked number 12 nationally in the Rally Obedience Top 20.

But perhaps the biggest coup for the humble team was the reaction of the judge who once questioned their obedience trial hopes. Not only did she give them a high score that she announced they had won outright, she also became their advocate, offering them private lessons. Ironically, however, she too had to face some criticism, as she began receiving numerous e-mails about her classes making disabled dogs perform!

The Rally O trials continued to interest Sapphire, but she, with her human companion's desire to keep the visually impaired canine involved with life, soon heeled into another passion—one that would not give her pause but honored her paws.

Pawsitive Therapy Troupe, registered with Therapy Dogs International and the Delta Society, became a part of Sapphire's life when she was two and a half. Trained to provide her healing presence (which animals so often naturally possess) to those in need, the Great Dane seemed to revel in the various places Jewel and she would frequent each week.

One was the Read-to-Me activity at local schools. Lying down beside the readers, Sapphire gave each problem reader her undivided attention as the elementary school children read aloud. Each seemed more at ease as they tackled the words on the pages in front of them with the dog nearby, especially a young boy from Germany. Though identified as having broken English, the brown-haired fourth grader read more confidently with Sapphire there. Finishing the book, the boy would reach over and ever so lightly touch Sapphire's head. In response, as if to tell him he wasn't broken, the dog would nudge closer to the youngster.

Visiting the elderly at senior homes, Sapphire was usually let off the leash, as the residents there preferred to play with her. With her noise-making computer chip toys that allowed her to track them, the canine fetched the playthings for her playmates. With the senior citizens, she could lick faces. Her touching was obviously most welcomed by the older people, whose smiling faces dominated the room. The Great Dane once told Jewel through Sharon that touching is special, and that old people don't get touched enough.

At the Veterans' Administration hospital, Sapphire once again used her animal-therapy skills. As she and the other dogs, along with their human companions, entered the Blind Center, she knew she was in a place where she could really relate to the patients. From those in their early 20s to senior citizens, the patients she visited had either already lost their sight or were losing their vision and were there to be trained to live with their disability.

Pulling Jewel gently along, Sapphire went to each one. She wanted them to know, as she communicated to Sharon Callahan recently during a session, that being different is not only okay, it's special. She also wanted them to know that she understands internal visions, the kind that she and Jewel share with each other, most notably in the agility classes.

Often Jewel, in talking with the blind at the hospital, told them about her animal companion's agility training. Always curious, they listened closely to what the dog must accomplish and how she was faring in the new classes, for with their blindness, they too had to go through agility and obstacles training. Jewel detailed some of the class demands: walking up and down the teeter-totter, a metal-framed obstacle with open sides that the Great Dane had to crawl through—today, she said, the frame was actually set up for smaller dogs, so Sapphire had to overcome that impediment as well—and an A-framed obstacle that Sapphire had to walk on. When someone asked how Jewel communicated with her dog, she answered that she used a clicker for auditory cues, but when it came to visual clues, she relied on the power of intent.

For example, when she walked into a trials' room set up for competition, she'd intend that Sapphire receive visual impressions of what Jewel was actually seeing. The intentions obviously worked. "But," Jewel asked, "why not? Everyone has experienced times when someone said exactly what you were thinking, so why can't someone see exactly what you're seeing?"

That night, in a session with the animal intuitive from Mt. Shasta, Jewel told Sharon about the visit to the Blind Center. Though she knew Sapphire had brought much into her life, she wasn't so much aware of the magnitude of those changes until today. Here she was, once so painfully shy she could melt into the walls, and now with her animal companion by her side, she was talking openly and assuredly about all kinds of things, like visual impressions. Jewel said she wanted to thank Sapphire for helping her to believe in herself and asked her if this learning was what her dear animal companion had been mirroring to her all along.

Jewel with Sapphire, the Great Dane

Merging with the Great Dane, Sharon said that Sapphire wanted Jewel to know that she didn't need to go through the animal intuitive to get that answer. She should just look (being a blind dog, Sapphire certainly couldn't do that for her, the dog teased) around her during the times when the two of them were out on their therapy visits. It was then that Jewel beamed back best what Sapphire had been diligently striving to reflect about and to her: her human companion not only understood the differences in all beings, especially one blind dog, but she honored and refused to discriminate against any of them. That is indeed a beautiful, untarnished reflection.

With the night slipping into early morning, Sharon typed out the last paragraph of her notes on Jewel and Sapphire's session. The dog's words today brought to mind the inspiring ending from *The Ugly Duckling*. The animal communicator knew them by heart: "He was very happy, but not at all proud, for a good heart never becomes proud. He thought of how he had been pursued and scorned, and now he heard them all say that he was the most beautiful of all beautiful birds."

20

REACH OUT
AND TOUCH

Something wonderful had happened:
he had actually reached out and
touched a badger in the wilds.

Incident at Hawk's Hill, Alan W. Eckert

Padding through the amber, crimson and burnt-orange leaves that carpeted the yard to her office at dawn, the animal intuitive smiled at the glory surrounding her. Her favorite time of year was here again. Like sleeveless blouses and sandals, summer had been put away. And the feeling she'd had since childhood, that of autumn being the start of a new year, engulfed her. From the vibrant colors to the crisp morning air, she soaked in the season's rich sensations.

Stopping to sit on the porch stoop for a moment before going inside to work, Sharon Callahan pulled her purple shawl around her. Close by, a squirrel with an acorn tucked in his mouth scooted up a tree. Following his path up the oak, she eyed a large brown spider. Fat with a sac of eggs, the spider was at the edge of a dew-moistened web that draped between the tree's lowest limb and a nearby bush.

Immediately, Sharon thought of Charlotte, as the memory of a beloved story threaded her thoughts like the web the spider created to save Wilbur the pig. Charlotte's example of serving another with love, and mirroring that for all to see in the barnyard, reminded Sharon of the many animals she had communicated with over the years, as well as the lessons about living and dying that they had reflected, and continued to reflect, to their human companions every day.

Suddenly, a grunt interrupted the animal communicator's thoughts. Emerging from the thick brush beside the building, a broad, heavy-bodied creature, weighing about thirty pounds, with thick grayish-reddish fur and a white stripe from his nose to his shoulders, headed for the woods. Walking on tiptoes that had sharp claws ready for serious digging, the animal had a rolling gait and moved with a steady purpose. Mystified, and yet not wanting to disturb him in any way, Sharon watched him a bit longer before she realized that he must surely be a badger. Just before he slipped into the woods, she respectfully merged with him, asking if she might talk to him a moment. As with any animal she hoped to communicate with, she would respect his decision and act accordingly.

Unresponsive at first, he messaged with thoughts and feelings that he only had time for a brief conversation, as he was a nocturnal creature who preferred to be away from the activity of the daytime. There was too much light and too much movement. Though he *was* curious about humans and how they seemed to like having activity and brightness around them all the time. Laughing aloud, Sharon agreed that human beings did have a propensity for both.

Communicating further, the badger also noted that many people seemed to have forgotten that there was another part of daily life. Away from the artificial lights of civilization, the nighttime had its own mystical light, whether from the moon, the stars, lightning or a firefly. The darkness also had its own rhythm. One that vibrated with intense energy, yet with a sense of stillness.

Acknowledging that the nighttime did have its own richness that she had not explored in awhile, Sharon vowed to the creature and herself that she would set aside some time to dwell in the sunless hours in the upcoming days. "Nights," the badger corrected her with humor, as he relayed to her that he had to head for his home, the hole that was his haven during the daylight hours.

Wishing him a good day, or rather a good night, she thanked him for communicating with her. Perhaps, she added, they would meet again and he could tell her more about his underground home, as she knew so little about it.

As his wedge-shaped body slowly entered the woods, he suddenly halted and turned back to look at her. Feeling a connection that went beyond thoughts and words, she locked eyes with him. For several moments, the badger held the connection. Then he turned back, resumed his exit from the open space and melted away into the dark woods.

Tingling with excitement, she hugged herself. Not only was he the first badger she'd ever communicated with, their rendezvous had also put before her once again one of the greatest gifts that animals contribute to humankind: through their love, they serve as compassionate mirrors, reflecting essential information that can help people see themselves clearly. Certainly the badger had done that for her by mirroring to her the forgotten joy of experiencing nature during nighttime's quiet serenity. His example of loving reflection unearthed a treasured line from a poem by Rumi, the 13th-century Persian poet: "Love is a mirror, it reflects only your essence, if you have the courage to look in its face."

The succinct encounter with Mr. Badger this morning, especially their eye embrace, also reinforced the reason that mirroring works so well: the unwavering spiritual connection between humans and animals. Rooted in the basic language of honor and love, the connection required no words, only the language of the heart. Of the thousands of readings she'd liaised over the past 20 years, most of the clients who'd called with concerns about their animal companions were aware of this unity, but were often wobbly as to how to translate this spiritual tie into an even tighter bond. They asked what they could do to become closer to their animal friends.

Leaning back on the step and pulling out a pad and a No. 2 pencil, Sharon thought about that request and what the badger had shown her today. With the day's end, she felt she would have some answers.

By the time the harvest moon beamed overhead that night upon her and she had closed the office door, the animal intuitive had a list of simple meditations. Gleaned from the wisdom of the animals she had communicated with and their stories of service, the meditations offered a way for people to communicate with all animals. To be practiced with an animal companion or with those in nature, the meditations were not only a template for reaching out and touching the heart of an animal, but they also spoke to core life issues for all.

As Sharon's footsteps landed lightly on the porch steps, she found herself slowing down, then stopping. Cocking her ear to her right, she leaned toward the wooded area behind the office and waited. Realizing she was listening for the sound of movement in the yard, or perhaps even a grunt, she held her breath. But no unusual sounds interjected themselves amid the night's normal activities.

Savoring her memory of the face-to-face encounter with the badger that morning, she walked toward home in the cool October night. Around her the leaves cascaded softly. She thought about the unexpected joy seeing the wild creature had brought to her and how he had inspired her to seek out the meditations to help others. As her thoughts lingered on the badger's gifts, Sharon recalled a sentence from a book she'd read in her early days. Though she'd enjoyed it then, on this beautiful autumn evening the words from *Incident at Hawk's Hill* seemed even more precious. "Something wonderful had happened: he had actually reached out and touched a badger in the wilds."

Meditations

1. "The Real Thing." Applauds the reason for all: love.

> Love transcends all limitations of time and space,
> And is instantly felt throughout the universe
> In all realms and dimensions
> Prayers thoughts and loving wishes are received even after death
> For the soul of the animal lives on
> And the soul feels, receives, and responds independently of the
>   body
> All whom we have loved are with us forever
> As close to us as our own breath.
> The animals teach the lessons of faith, hope, and love
> And the greatest is Love, for after all is said and done . . .
> Love alone remains.

2. "The Bond." Aids in keeping the bond between you and your animal companion vital and full of compassionate energy.

> Each day and each moment of life I am born anew.
> Each day and each moment of life my animal companion is
> Born anew.
> I look to each moment as a rebirth and I allow my
> Relationship with my animal to be born anew in each moment.
> I hold no one to my past perception of them. I give each
>   person, each animal
> And each situation the gift of new life in each moment.
> Each moment I view the world like a freshly hatched chick.

3. "A Passion for Living." Assists in keeping the enthusiasm for life and life's purposes alive.

> It is often said that the only constant in life is change
> I accept that change is as natural as life itself.
> I watch in awe the great lesson animals teach
> About adaptability while accepting that at times
> My cherished animal companion may have difficulty
> With change as I do for he/she has become much like me.
> I honor and bless the sacred bond of friendship with my
> Animal companion and I vow to offer assistance and
> Comfort during life's trying times as he/she so willingly
> Offers me comfort.
> We will help one another keep the faith . . . all is well.

4. "Pure Motives." Reconnects with life's blueprint and good intentions.

> When I feel no clear direction
> I turn within the silent sanctuary of my heart,
> Knowing that the Divine Plan is working in and through me
>   every moment
> Though it may not be apparent.
> I remember that it is in giving that I receive
> And I keep ever watchful for ways to be of service
> As the Great Universal Intelligence ever serves me.

I honor the animals and all the ways in which they serve
   humankind
And I strive to be of service in any way I am able.

5. "Following the Heart's Lead." Attends to listening and staying on
course with the heart.

In the still, silent sanctuary of my own heart
The answer to every question appears.
From the quiet sanctuary of my heart
I hear the voice of my animal companion.
From this great well of silence
I connect with the silent loving heart of every
Being . . . and God Itself.
As my heart connects with the Heart of All
I know the appropriate action to take
In each moment of life.
Here in the deep silence of my being
I have all that I will ever need.

6. "Good Thoughts." Helps in staying mindful of the power of
believing and trusting in the best.

The Universe is user-friendly.
All that happens, happens in my best interest.
All that I experience within myself,
In relation with other people or
In relationship with my beloved animal companion
Is teaching me what I need most to know.
I trust the Universe is providing for me perfectly
In each moment . . . all is well.

7. "Friendship." Acknowledges the beauty of friendships.

A true heart friend is the greatest joy in life.
I honor all the special friends life has brought my way . . .
Whether feathered . . . furred . . . finned . . . skinned or taloned.
Love and friendship come in many forms.
I honor and bless all the forms friendship takes as
My loving animal companion;
The hawk whose heavenward flight catches my eye

When I need a lift;
The butterfly who shares appreciation of the beauty of my
    garden;
The spider whose shimmering web decorates my window sill.
I receive the friendship of the Universe without a need to covet
Or grasp, knowing that friendship fills my days if I but open my
Eyes and see its myriad forms.
I understand that the deepest forms of friendship often arise in
The silent communion of hearts.

8. "Keeping the Faith." Reminds that faith is beyond all obstacles, disappointments and sorrow.

Let Sorrow redeem itself. Keep shiningly sorrowful, and
    within the great well of
Your being will spring
The fountain of joy.
All obstacles are overcome in the silent sanctuary of stillness.
I allow my animal companion to teach me the lesson of
    overcoming . . .
That sorrow leads to joy and joy springs forth from giving.
When sorrow overcomes me I look for ways to give
And soon sorrow gives way to joy

9. "Living in the Here and Now." Addresses how to live in the moment without worry, fear and other negative thoughts and actions.

As I follow the lead of my animal companion,
I fully enter the sacredness of the present moment
From the perspective of this sacred moment of now
All is whole and complete . . . no past, no future
Just the moment of now . . . whole and complete as it is.

10. "Aging with Grace." Addresses growing older with wisdom.

Everything that is born must age and die,
For this is the nature of life on earth.
I can learn much about gracefully transitioning through
The stages of life by observing the cycles of nature and
The life of my beloved animal companion, for he is teaching me
The lesson of aging with grace.

Is he not as beautiful in his old age as in his youth?
Is there not a richness at the end of his life not found in its
    beginning?
As I watch my companion age with grace, accepting each day,
    each
Season, each year on his own terms, I learn to age with grace
    myself.
Taking his lead, I accept each season of life gracefully,
    knowing that
Each has its beauty and that one cannot exist without the other.
I know that at the end of life I, my animal companion and all
    that lives
Will be enfolded back into the arms of God.

11. "Loss and Grief." Honors the passing of a being and soothes the
    pain of grief and loss.

My grief is a testament to the love I shared with my animal
    companion.
To ease the pain of loss surrounding the death of my beloved
    friend
And to honor his/her life
I offer up my love and gratitude for the gifts received during
    our time together
As a healing prayer for all the animals
Especially those who die with no one to grieve their passing.
I transform my grief into a sacramental blessing of the whole
    kingdom of animals.
I know by doing this my grief will turn to joy, for this is the
    alchemy of the heart.
Turning my grief outward as a prayer, I take the focus off
    myself
And the whole universe and all the beings who dwell within it
    smile in thanksgiving.
Sorrow is ever making way for joy.

12. "Lighten Up." Encourages joy, humor and living life with a light heart.

> A heart that is light is a heart full of light.
> I allow my animal companion to teach me the lesson of
>   lightening up.
> Even in times of hardship and sorrow, the world is a beautiful
>   place.
> I give myself permission to dance and sing . . .
> A dance of hardship . . .
> A dance of sorrow . . .
> A dance of joy . . .
> A dance of life in all its glory.
> I receive the teaching of the animals.
> I allow my body to express what I am feeling in my heart.

13. "On Being Different." Honors the beauty of all beings.

> I am unique and perfect.
> I have been called to earth to deliver a special gift that only I
>   can give.
> I am a light in the world, a beautifully colored thread in the
>   tapestry of life,
> A rich note in the symphony of life without which the earth
>   would be incomplete.
> No one else has my special color, light and note.
> Like me, my animal companion has her own special light,
>   color and note
> As important and unique as mine.
> If she or I are considered imperfect by the world, I am assured
>   that God
> Creates only masterpieces, and that we are masterpieces.
> Together we combine our gifts to add beauty to the world,
> Gifts that only we can bring.

Wild Clover on Mt. Shasta.

PURUSHA ANANDA

Epilogue

I knew from the beginning of researching and writing this book that I would dedicate it to Jerry; what I didn't know was that my feline friend would leave once our work was completed. Six days after the manuscript was finished, Jerry passed away in my arms. A mirror of the brightest light, he was indeed a reflection of that which is noble in all of us.

Resources

Chapter Quotes References

Andersen, Hans Christian. *The Ugly Duckling.* New York: Scribner, 1965.

Armstrong, William Howard. *Sounder.* New York: Harper & Row, 1969.

Bach, Richard. *Jonathan Livingston Seagull.* New York: Macmillan, 1970.

Bianco, Margery Williams. *The Velveteen Rabbit.* New York: Holt, Rinehart and Winston, 1983.

Boone, J. Allen. *Kinship With All Life.* New York: Harper, 1954.

Burnett, Frances Hodgson. *A Little Princess.* Philadelphia: Lippincott, 1963.

Carroll, Lewis. *Alice's Adventures in Wonderland.* Cambridge, Mass.: Candlewick Press, 1999.

————. *Through the Looking Glass.* New York: Random House, 1946.

Eckert, Allan W. *Incident at Hawk's Hill.* Boston: Little Brown, 1971.

Farley, Walter. *The Black Stallion.* New York: Random House, 1941.

Leaf, Munro. *The Story of Ferdinand.* New York: The Viking Press, 1936.

Morey, Walt. *Gentle Ben.* New York: Dutton, 1965.

Rawlings, Marjorie Kinnan. *The Yearling.* New York: C. Scribner's Sons, 1938.

Sanchez-Silva, Jose Maria. *The Boy and the Whale.* New York: McGraw-Hill, 1964.

Saunders, Marshall. *Beautiful Joe.* Racine, Wisc.: Whitman Publishing Company, 1965.

Sewell, Anna. *Black Beauty.* New York: DK Pub., 1997.

White, E. B. *Charlotte's Web.* New York: HarperCollins, 1980.

Animal Companion Resources

The following resources are offered from Animal Intuitive Sharon Callahan. Gleaned from her personal experiences, they aim to serve as a guide to having a better understanding and healthier, happier life with our animal companions.

Books

Boone, J. Allen. *The Language of Silence.* New York: Harper & Row, 1970.

Callahan, Sharon. *Healing Animals Naturally With Flower Essences and Intuitive Listening.* Mt. Shasta, Calif.: Sacred Spirit Publishing, 2001.

Carmack, Betty J. *Grieving the Death of a Pet.* Minneapolis: Augsburg Books, 2003.

Clothier, Susan. *Bones Would Rain from the Sky, Deepening Our Relationships with Dogs.* New York: Warner Books, 2002.

Galico, Paul. *The Small Miracle.* Garden City, N.Y.: Doubleday, 1952.

Goodall, Jane, and Marc Bekoff. *The Ten Trusts: What We Must Do to Care for the Animals We Love.* San Francisco: HarperSanFrancisco, 2002.

Goldstein, Robert, and Susan. *Dr. Bob and Susan Goldstein's Guide to Wellness and Longevity for Dogs and Cats.* Neptune City, N.J.: TFH Publications, 2004.

Holloway, Sage. *Animal Healing and Vibrational Medicine.* Nevada City, Calif.: Blue Dolphin, 2001.

Kowalski, Gary. *The Souls of Animals.* Walpole, N.H.: Stillpoint, 1991.

Lauck, Joanne Elizabeth. *The Voice of the Infinite in the Small: Revisioning the Insect-Human Connection.* Mill Springs, N.C.: Swan Raven, 1998.

Lewis, C. S. *The Complete Chronicles of Narnia.* New York: HarperCollins, 2002.

McElroy, Susan Chernak. *Animals As Guides for the Soul.* New York: Ballantine, Wellspring, 1998.

———. *Animals As Teachers and Healers.* New York: Ballantine, 1997.

————. *Heart in the Wild: A Journey of Self-Discovery with Animals in the Wilderness.* New York: Ballantine, 2002.

Midkiff, Mary D. *She Flies Without Wings: How Horses Touch a Woman's Soul.* New York: Delacorte Press, 2001

Reynolds, Rita. *Blessing the Bridge: What Animals Have to Teach Us About Death, Dying and Beyond.* Troutdale, Ore.: New Sage Press, 2001.

Sarton, May. *The Fur Person.* New York: W. W. Norton, 1983.

Saunders, Marshall. *Beautiful Joe's Paradise.* Halifax, Nova Scotia: Formac Publishing, 2001.

Schoen, Allen. *Kindred Spirits.* New York: Broadway Books, 2001.

————. *Love, Miracles and Animal Healing.* New York: Simon & Schuster, 1995.

Sheldrake, Rupert. *Dogs That Know When Their Owners Are Coming Home: And Other Unexplained Poems of Animals.* New York: Crown, 1999.

Sheridan, Kim. *Animals and the Afterlife: True Stories of Our Best Friends' Journey Beyond Death.* Escindido, Calif.: EnLighthouse Publishing, 2003.

Grief and Loss Support

www.anaflora.com: *Anaflora:* Animal death and grieving support, stories, prayer and perpetual memorial pages.

www.pet-loss.net: *Companion Animal Grief and Loss Support:* A state-by-state guide to support groups, counselors and animal cemeteries. Moira Anderson Allen, D.V.M.

www.rabbit.org: *Companion Rabbit Loss Support:* Assists with care, rescue and loss of rabbits.

www.animalsandtheafterlife.com: Author Kim Sheridan's site for submitting stories of animal loss and after life.

www.thegabrielfoundation.org: *The Gabriel Foundation:* Rescue, care sanctuary for parrots.

Holistic Animal Care

Veterinary

American Holistic Veterinary Medical Association
2218 Old Emmorton Road
Bel Air, MD 21015
410-569-0795
www.AHVMA.com

Robert Goldstein, D.V.M.
606 Post Road East
Westport, CT 06880
914-533-5162
www.healingcenterforanimals.com

Allen Schoen, D.V.M., M.S.
30 Old Quarry Road
Ridgefield, CT 06877
203-438-8878 or 860-354-2287
www.askdrschoen.com

Lori Tapp, D.V.M.
222 Old Gibbs Road
Weaverville, NC 28787
828-658-8496
www.drtapp.com

Charles Loops, D.V.M.
38 Waddell Hollow
Pittsboro, NC 27312
919-542-0442
www.charlesloopsdvm.com

Joel Murphy, D.V.M.
34820 US 19
Palm Harbor, FL 34684
727-784-0558
www.pethealing.org

Animal Well-Being Consultants

Susan Goldstein, Animal Well-Being Consultant
Earth Animal Healing Center
606 Post Road East
Westport, CT 06880
914-533-5162
www.earthanimal.com

Natural Animal Care and Nutrition for Dogs and Cats
www.earthanimal.com

Anaflora Flower Essence Therapy for Animals
P.O. Box 1056
Mt. Shasta, CA 96067
www.anaflora.com

Periodicals

Animal Wellness magazine
Dana Cox, Publisher/Editor
419 George Street North
Peterborough, Ontario, Canada
K9H 3R4
888-466-5266
www.animalwellnessmagazine.com

Journal of Interspecies Telepathic Communication
World-wide list of animal communicators
Pegasus Publishing
P.O. Box 1060
Point Reyes, CA 94956
415-663-1247
www.animaltalk.net

Love of Animals newsletter
Dr. Bob and Susan Goldstein, Publishers
606 Post Road East
Westport, CT 06880
800-211-6365